WELCOME

IN THE past 20 years rugby union has grown almost out of all proportion. The catalyst has been the move to make the game professional (in 1995), after more than a century as an amateur sport, so hopefully the time is right for a book that is aimed at its legion of new fans.

We hope we have struck the balance in making it an attractive proposition for people who have enjoyed rugby union for many years and those who are just stumbling across our great sport.

No project like this could ever come together without a huge team effort and my thanks go to a number of other people, who have worked tirelessly on *Rugby: A New Fan's Guide*. Jamie Latchford's design work has been exemplary and his dedication admirable and the same can be said for the work of Linda Carroll, cover designer James Watson and the best proofreader in the rugby world, Alan Pearey.

Over at A&C Black where they championed the project, Corinne Roberts kicked it all off, Charlotte Atyeo took over at the end of the first quarter and without Lucy Beevor it would simply never have happened.

The book is taken to another level by the incredible rugby photographs from Getty Images, which richly illustrate the pages. Their library just seems to get better and better.

And as always my thanks go to my wife Jo, who is a constant source of inspiration and enthusiasm, a feat in itself considering a young lady called Elodie appeared in our lives at the start of 2007. This book is dedicated to my girls!

As with any book packed with statistics, there may be one or two errors along the way and I would be grateful if you would email me at *Rugby World magazine* (paul_morgan@ipcmedia.com), where I am editor, with any you find, or with suggestions or comments that could improve a future edition.

I hope you enjoy it!

PAUL MORGAN
Editor

CONTENTS

PAUL MORGAN

RUGBY

A NEW FAN'S GUIDE TO THE GAME, THE TEAMS AND THE PLAYERS

First published 2008 by
A & C Black Publishers Ltd
38 Soho Square, London W1D 3HB
www.acblack.com

ISBN 978-1-408-10375-3

A CIP catalogue record for this book is available from the British Library.

Designed and typeset in BentonSans by Jamie Latchford
Cover photographs of Danny Cipriani and James Hook © Action Images
Cover photographs of Brian O'Driscoll and Chris Paterson © Corbis
Inside photographs © Getty Images

This book is produced using paper that is made from wood grown in managed, sustainable forests. It is natural, renewable and recyclable. The logging and manufacturing processes conform to the environmental regulations of the country of origin.

Printed and bound in China

122
46
56
88
118

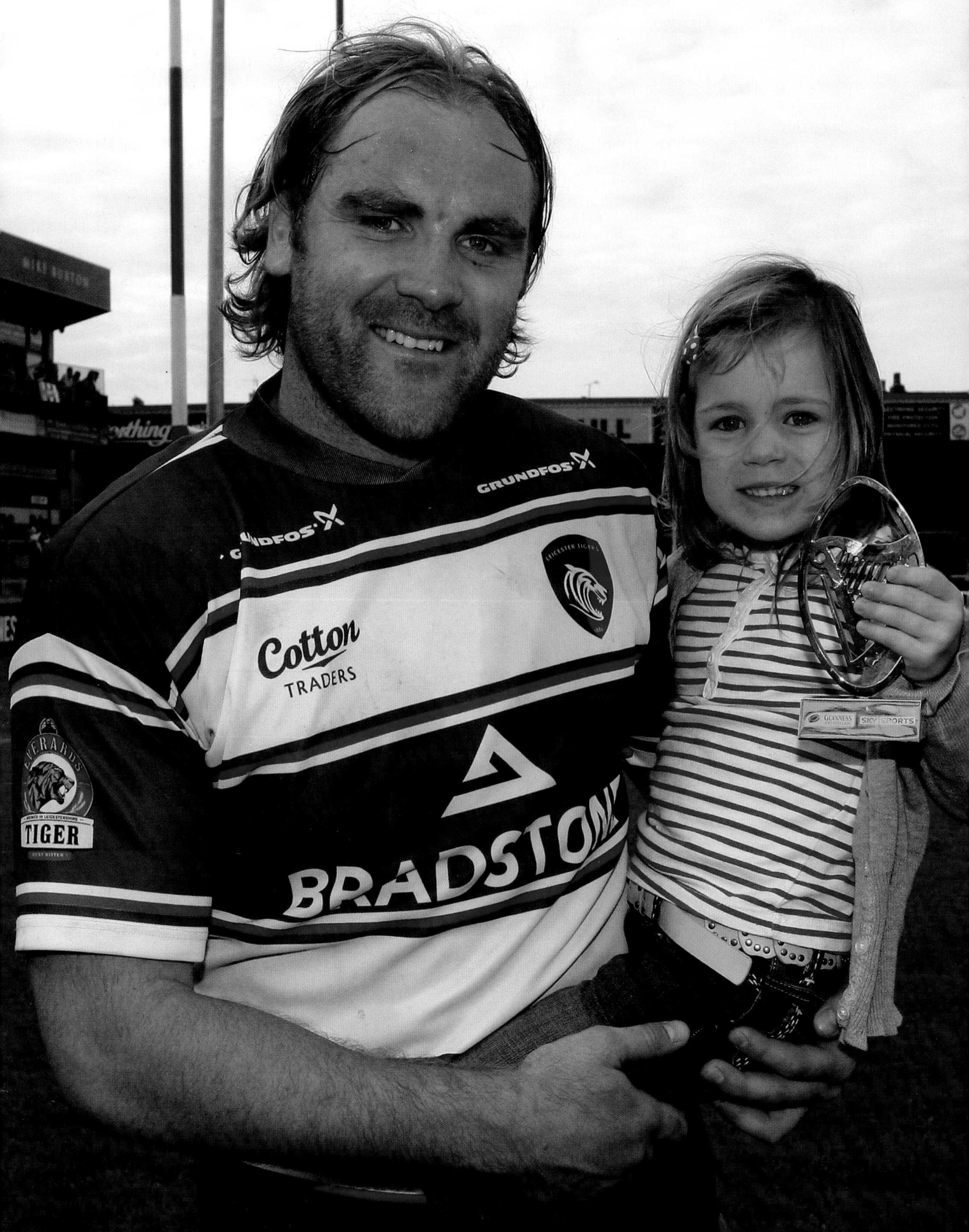
GRUNDFOS
GRUNDFOS
Cotton
TRADERS
BRADSTONE
TIGER

THE BIG KICK-OFF

THE GREATEST TEAM sport in the world is how rugby union is described by the tens of millions of people across the world who love the game.

It is famously depicted as a sport that is for 'all shapes and sizes'. No matter whether you are 5ft 2in, or 6ft 8in, 10 stone or 20 stone, there is a place for you in the great game of rugby union as the big and the small come together.

It is a family-friendly sport, whether in the world of mini-rugby, where youngsters start the game at seven years of age, or in the professional game. Reputations and medals may be on the line with the pros but ▶

THE BIG KICK-OFF

▶ they still have time for a beer and a chat after the match, as camaraderie amongst players, coaches and supporters is one of the platforms on which the game was built.

Modern-day rugby has three main forms: 15-a-side, the fast growing seven-a-side and the less often seen ten-a-side rugby, all drawing their own hordes of followers. The 15-a-side version of course takes centre stage most of the year but sevens, which has an annual IRB-run World Series and a World Cup, and tens have their place in the rugby calendar.

Rugby prides itself on being an inclusive sport. Women are ▶

Seven-a-side rugby is part of the Commonwealth Games...

...while wheelchair rugby is in the Olympics

THE FUNDAMENTALS

1 A GAME of rugby union lasts no longer than 80 minutes plus time lost and extra time if applicable. It is divided into two halves each of not more than 40 minutes' playing time. If time expires after a try is scored the referee allows the conversion kick.

TIME DIFFERENCE

2 RUGBY IS one of the few ball games where the ball cannot be passed forwards, although it can be kicked forwards. You must pass the ball either along or behind an imaginary line running at right angles to the side of the pitch.

PASS IT BEHIND YOU

3 RUGBY UNION is played with an oval-shaped ball. All balls must be between 28cm and 30cm in length. Full-size balls must weigh between 410 and 440 grams, while balls of different sizes may be used for matches between young players.

BALL SKILLS

4 TACKLING IS the main way of bringing an opponent down. But when you tackle an opponent, you cannot make contact with them above the shoulders. This is for safety reasons. See www.irb.com for all laws.

HIT HARD AND LOW

The 15-a-side game, where South Africa became world champions in 2007, is the crown jewel of rugby union

ESSENCE OF THE GAME

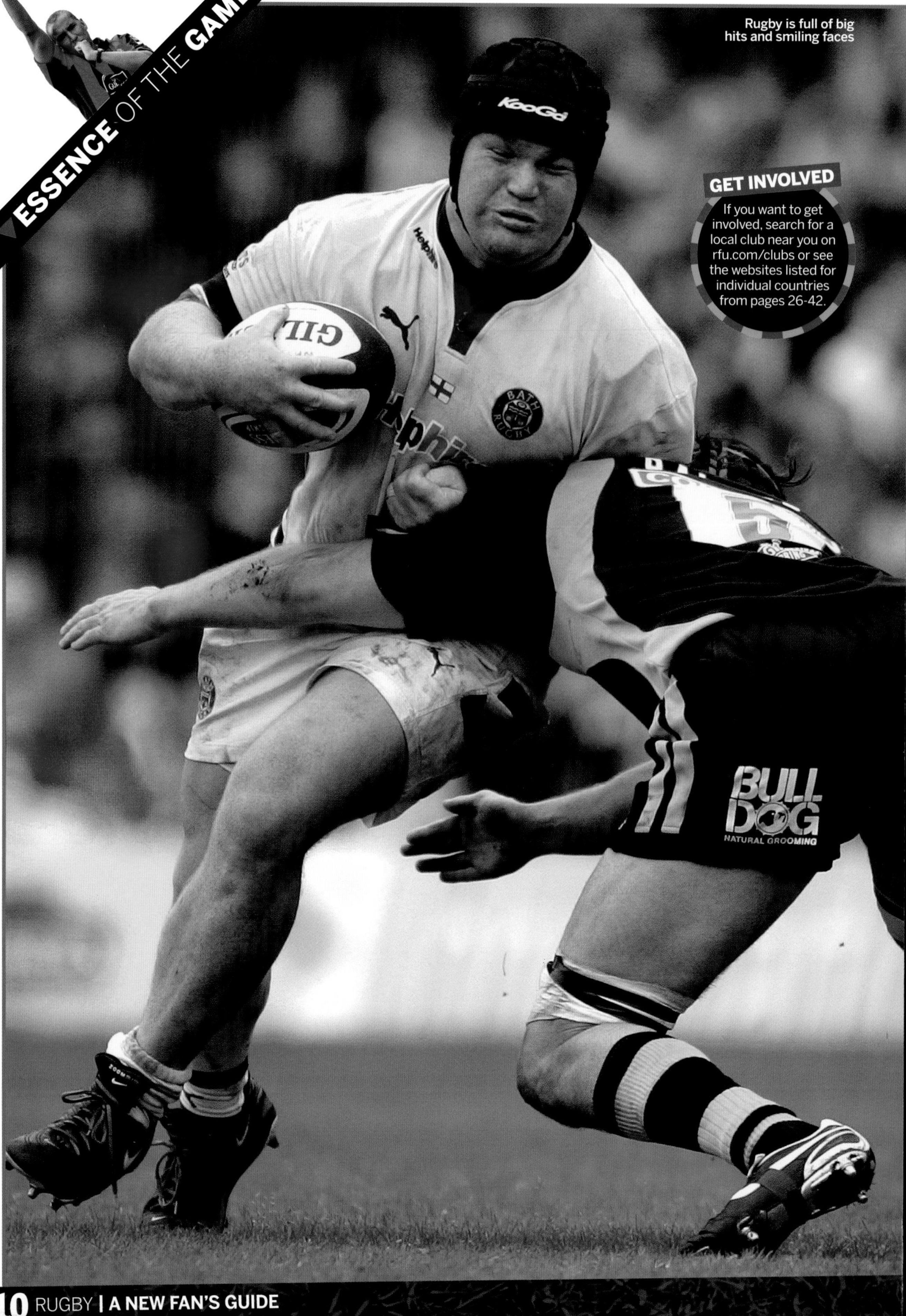

Rugby is full of big hits and smiling faces

GET INVOLVED

If you want to get involved, search for a local club near you on rfu.com/clubs or see the websites listed for individual countries from pages 26-42.

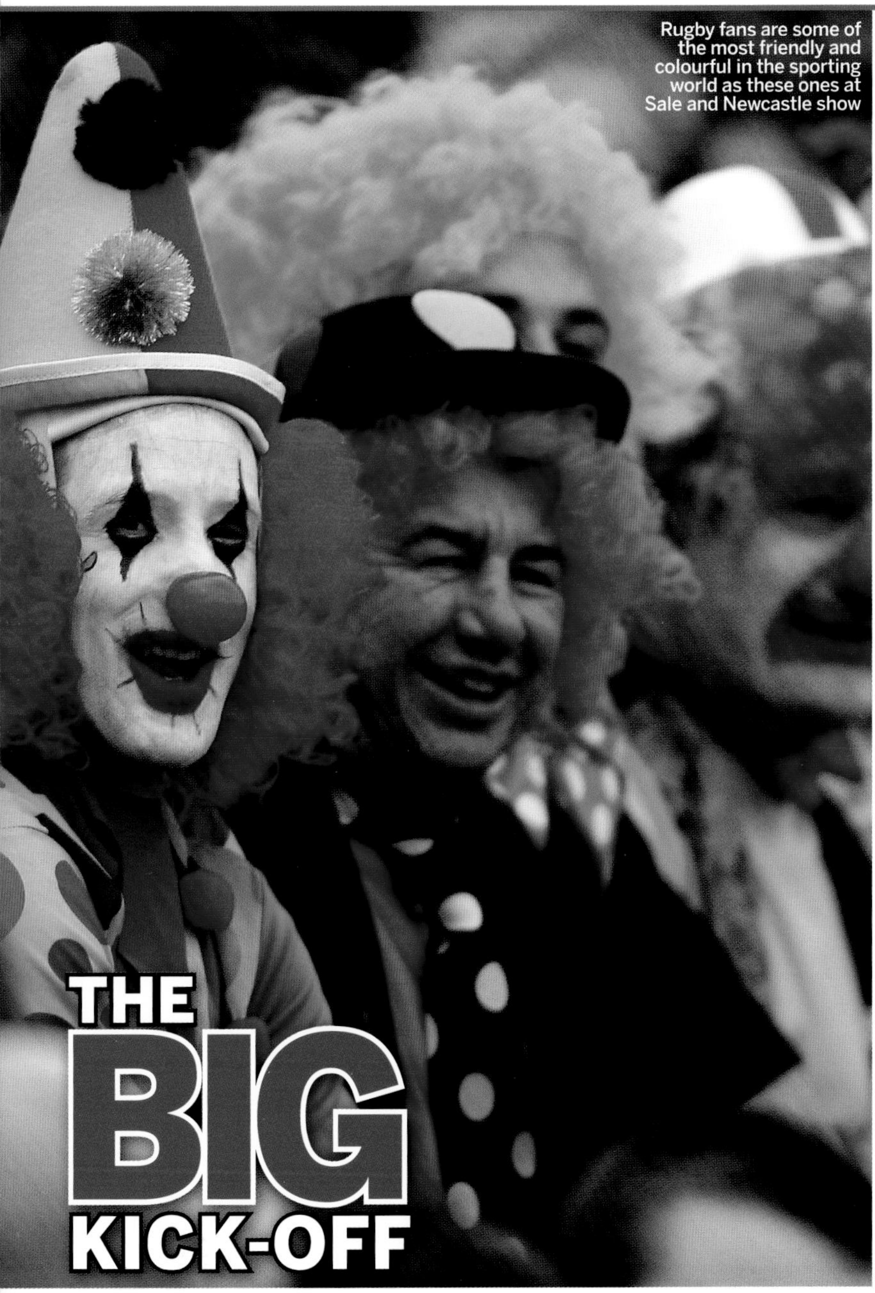

Rugby fans are some of the most friendly and colourful in the sporting world as these ones at Sale and Newcastle show

THE BIG KICK-OFF

▶ welcomed into the game, rugby for the deaf has Wales as world champions and, in the Olympics, wheelchair rugby is a featured sport, with a prized gold medal. The sexes are also mixed in the increasingly popular touch rugby, while at a younger age players also take part in tag rugby.

On the surface rugby union, at all levels, is a complicated game but those who take the trouble to understand its intricacies usually fall in love with a sport that lives and breathes on and off the field.

You can't fully enjoy rugby union without appreciating the social side of the game, where lifetime friendships are forged. There is never any need to segregate supporters as in other sports, and many rugby fans enjoy a pie and a pint in the bar (before and after the game!) as much as they love the match itself.

The tour is one of the mainstays of rugby union, like it is in cricket. Most clubs wouldn't contemplate a rugby season without a tour at the start, the end and sometimes in the middle. And as the years pass by teams are travelling further and further each season, spreading the word of the great game of rugby union across the planet.

RUGBY EQUIPMENT GUIDE

To play rugby union it's important you get kitted out correctly. **Players wear...**

1. MOUTHGUARD

2. HEADGEAR

3. BOOTS

4. BODY PROTECTION

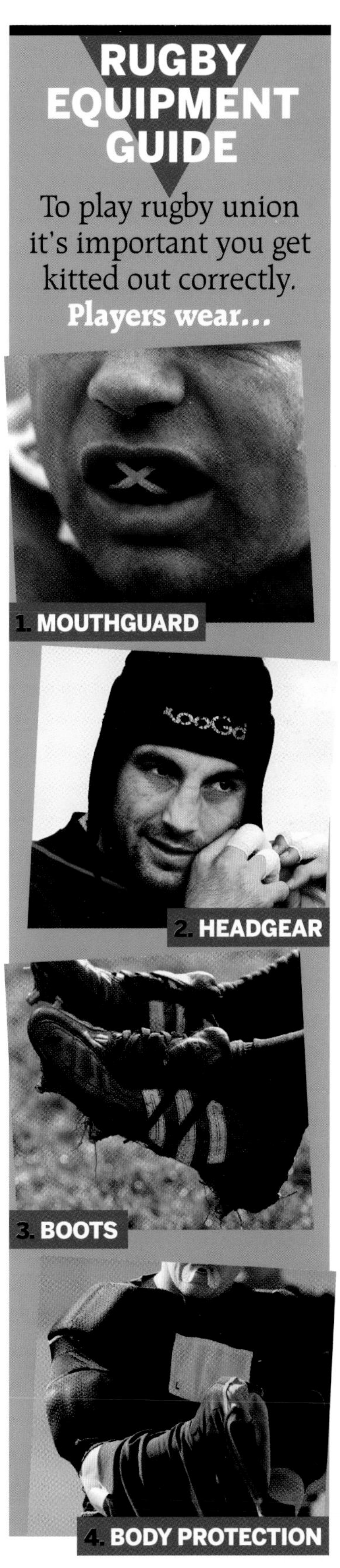

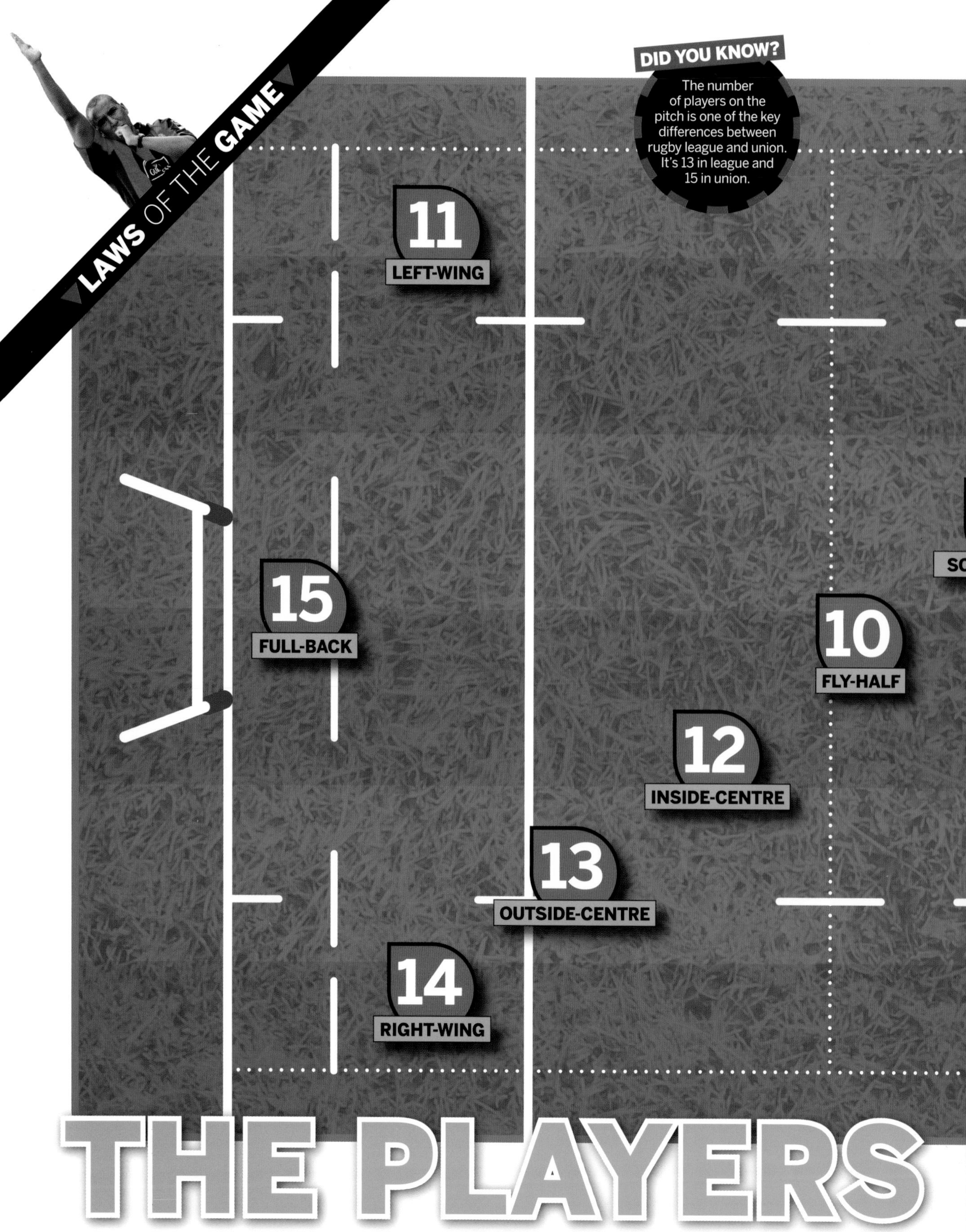

THE PLAYERS

Rugby started off in the late 19th century as a 20-a-side sport. But as the game developed the numbers reduced to the current 15, all with different, but equally important, jobs to perform.

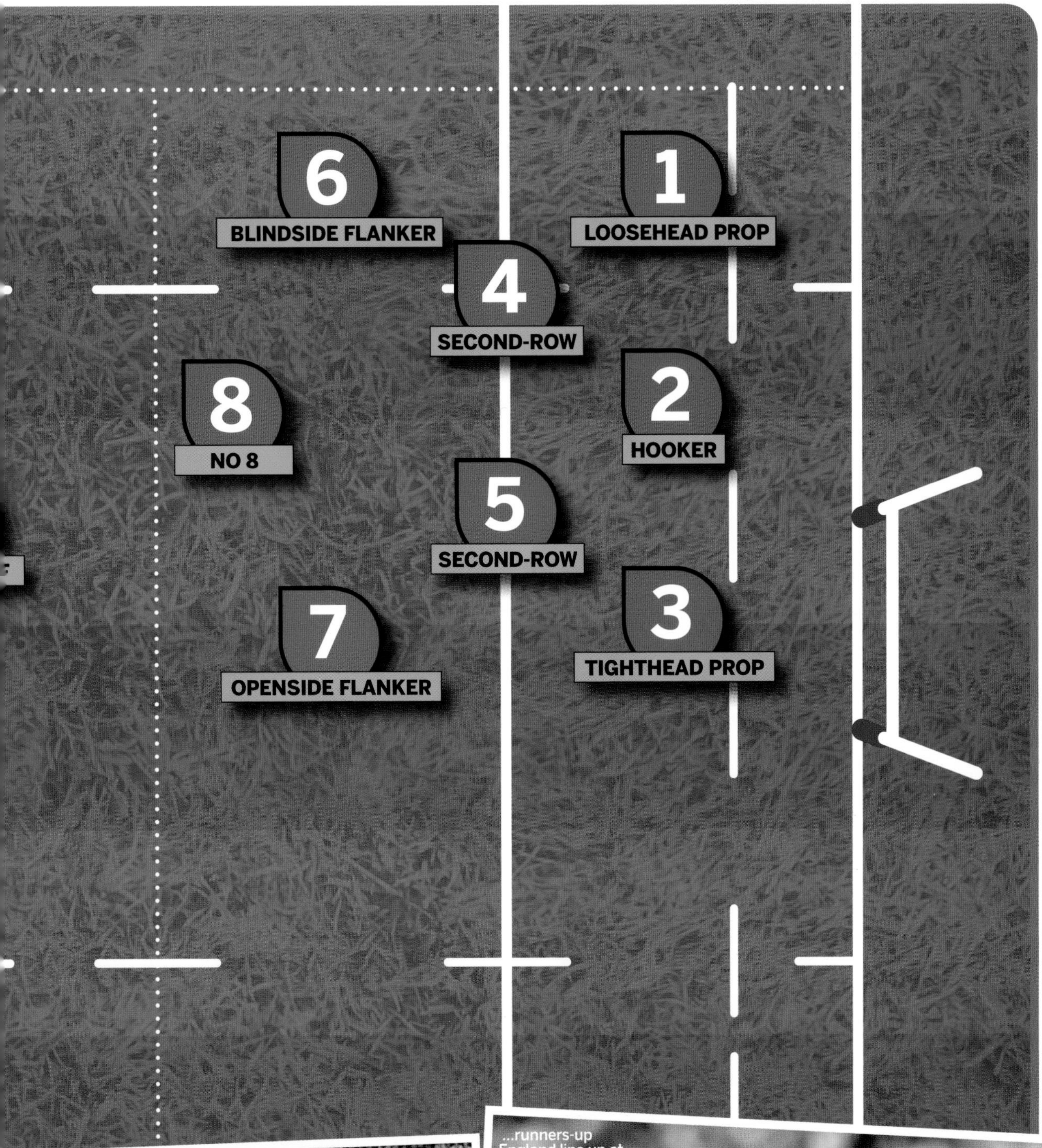

6 BLINDSIDE FLANKER

1 LOOSEHEAD PROP

4 SECOND-ROW

8 NO 8

2 HOOKER

5 SECOND-ROW

7 OPENSIDE FLANKER

3 TIGHTHEAD PROP

Winners South Africa and...

...runners-up England line up at the 2007 World Cup

DID YOU KNOW?

In rugby union sides are allowed to have seven substitutes and all can take the field. They are often split into four forwards and three backs.

THE PLAYERS

11 LEFT-WING

JUST LIKE the right-wing, the man on the left needs speed to burn. A kicking game will help but doing the 100 metres in less than 11 seconds is far more important. Expected to be there to finish off the moves.

Great player: Jonah Lomu

15 FULL-BACK

THE LAST line of defence, the full-back must be a fearless defender, who needs to be capable of sparking an attack. Over the years many have made a living as goalkickers as well.

Great player: Serge Blanco

10 FLY-HALF

RUGBY'S quarterback, most teams will live or die on the decisions of their outside-half. Needs to direct operations, set the game plan and run the show. Most are the side's frontline goalkickers.

Great player: Jonny Wilkinson

14 RIGHT-WING

THE QUICKEST player on the field, the least experienced of the two wings can often find themselves on the right as it can be easier to carry the ball in the right hand when attacking. Must be elusive.

Great player: Gerald Davies

9 SCRUM-HALF

THE GENERAL of all good rugby teams, it all starts with the scrum-half as they distribute the ball from the set-pieces and breakdowns. The best ones are aggressive, speedy and have an eye for a gap.

Great player: Gareth Edwards

13 OUTSIDE-CENTRE

THE QUICKER of the two centres, the outside man is normally the one looking to make the breaks and use the space created by his partner. Needs the bulk to break the line and determination in defence.

Great player: Philippe Sella

1 LOOSEHEAD PROP

THE PROP on the left-hand side of the scrum, they need to be as strong as an ox but in the modern game also able to pass and carry the ball. Has an important role lifting in the lineout.

Great player: Jason Leonard

12 INSIDE-CENTRE

OFTEN THE second outside-half in a side, the inside-centre will need to be bigger than the No 10 as he will have less time with the ball so will often need to take it into contact. A kicking game is crucial.

Great player: Will Greenwood

2 HOOKER

THEIR KEY roles are at the set-piece; scrummaging and hooking the ball back in the scrum and throwing in at the lineout. No side can prosper if these two crucial jobs go wrong.

Great player: Sean Fitzpatrick

THE POINTS SCORING SYSTEM IN RUGBY IS A LITTLE MORE COMPLICATED THAN IN FOOTBALL

1 A TRY
Five points
A TRY is scored when a player touches the ball down inside the opposition's in-goal area between the try line and dead ball line.

2 A CONVERSION
Two points
AFTER a team has scored a try (including a penalty try), they are awarded a conversion kick.

3 A PENALTY
Three points
A PENALTY kick is awarded after the opposition have committed one of a range of offences and the kicker can go for the posts from anywhere on the field.

4 A DROP GOAL
Three points
A DROP goal is scored when a player kicks the ball from hand through the posts. The ball is dropped to the ground and is kicked just after it has bounced.

3 TIGHTHEAD PROP

THE STRONG man of the team, the tighthead stands on the right-hand side of the scrum and takes the brunt of the opposition's drive. He is the rock on which great sides are made.

Great player: Carl Hayman ▶

4 SECOND-ROW Front Jumper

NEEDS TO be athletic enough to win more than their share of ball in the lineout, strong enough to push in the scrum, fit enough to get around the field and be a menace in the loose.

Great player: John Eales ▶

5 SECOND-ROW Middle Jumper

VERY SIMILAR role to the front jumper as these two guys form a partnership on which great forward packs are born. Has slightly more time to react at lineout time.

Great player: Martin Johnson ▶

6 BLINDSIDE

THE SILENT assassin, this guy gets through more of the unseen work on a rugby field than any other position. Must be as fit as anyone in the side as they have a crucial role in defence and attack.

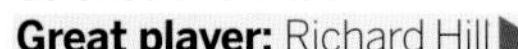

Great player: Richard Hill ▶

7 OPENSIDE

THEIR JOB is to make the opposition outside-half's life a misery while being there at every breakdown to contest the ball and set their side in attack. Often the defensive leader, they must have speed of thought.

Great player: Michael Jones ▶

8 NO 8

OFTEN THE hard yards merchant, they need to make the short gains around the breakdown. The link between backs and forward, a great No 8 also needs distribution skills and can have a big lineout role.

Great player: Dean Richards ▶

THE KICK-OFF

When the RFU was formed in 1871 there were 22 clubs present including Harlequin FC, Richmond, Belsize Park, Civil Service, Guy's Hospital and Blackheath.

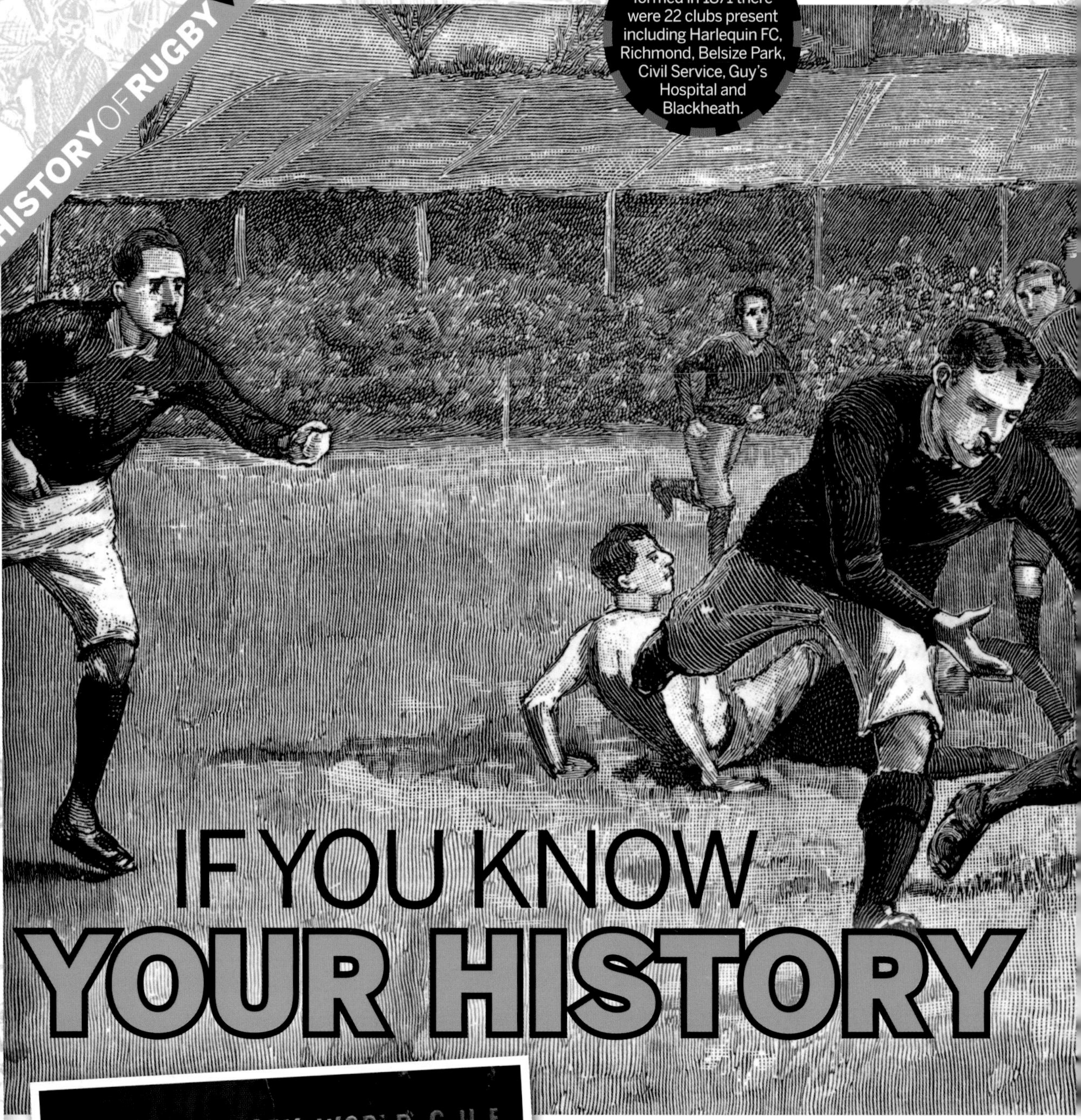

IF YOU KNOW YOUR HISTORY

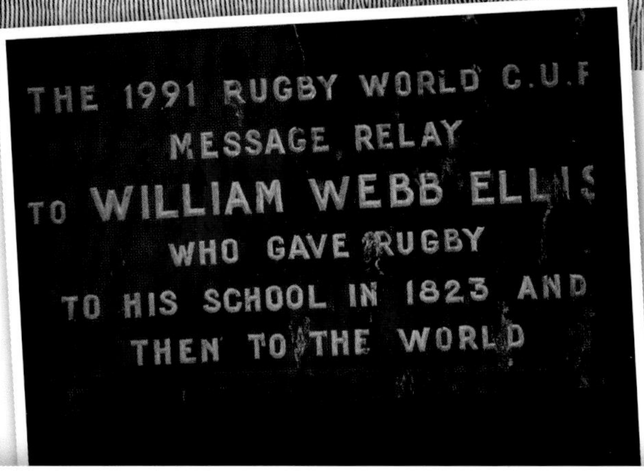

THE 1991 RUGBY WORLD C.U.P
MESSAGE RELAY
TO WILLIAM WEBB ELLIS
WHO GAVE RUGBY
TO HIS SCHOOL IN 1823 AND
THEN TO THE WORLD

Rugby union has a rich and varied history, spreading from humble beginnings across the world, loved by those who play it and admired by many who don't. Let us take you on a journey through more than 150 years of history, years on which the great game of rugby union was founded.

The Policeman who stands in the way.

A very early game of rugby union

RUGBY UNION is played in more than 100 countries across the world under a common set of laws (or rules) that have been developed by the International Rugby Board (IRB), the game's equivalent of FIFA in soccer.

Established in 1886 by the member unions, the IRB takes all the major worldwide decisions in the game. It currently has 96 full member unions (116 in total) from Albania to Australia and from Bosnia to Brazil, although only a select band of the biggest countries get a vote on the major issues.

The first international match was played in 1871 when Scotland beat England, but as you might imagine the game today is unrecognisable from that inaugural one that took place in Inverleith! For one thing the teams were 20-a-side and there were a number of laws most people wouldn't even believe, like hacking, which allowed players to whack each other in the shins.

Unfortunately for those who love a good story, it seems unlikely that a young man called William Webb Ellis 'picked up the ball and ran with it' to start rugby union, as many people say. The facts point to this being merely a myth and rugby historians like Jed Smith (former ▶

IF YOU KNOW YOUR HISTORY

▶ of the World Rugby Museum at Twickenham), John Griffiths and Stuart Farmer place little credibility against the story, especially as it didn't surface until decades later.

Rugby School in Warwickshire can, however, take great credit for the birth of the game as there is little doubt about the huge role this school played in the early years.

As Smith explains, it is likely that rugby developed in an evolutionary fashion from the many games that were being played at Rugby School at the time, with senior members of the school meeting at the end of each day to discuss developments. The fact that the Webb Ellis story only came to light many years after rugby kicked off probably confirms that it was nothing more than a story.

Rugby School old boys, or Rugbeians as they are known, played a huge role because so many of them travelled around the world after finishing school to spread the word about this new sport and try to get others to 'give it a try'. In 1871 a set of common rules were devised through the formation of the Rugby Football Union (RFU) in London, and soon afterwards that the first Test match followed, with victory for Scotland. Soon countries as far afield as New Zealand, South Africa and Australia were embracing this new game and it wasn't long before it made the short journey to France.The journey wasn't completed until a painful

TRUE VALUES

When points scoring started in rugby in 1890 the try was worth one point. It moved to three in 1899, four in 1971, and to its current five in 1992.

Rugby league evolved after the split of 1895

The World Cup started with a Kiwi win in 1987

KEY RUGBY DATES

1841 - Running with the ball was officially allowed in Rugby School's rules, providing the ball was taken on the bound; passing was specifically forbidden.

1862 - The spherical shaped ball evolves into one more resembling an egg as today.

1871 - The Rugby Football Union is formed and later that year the first international match is played, with Scotland beating England. Each side has 20, comprising 13 forwards, three half-backs, one three-quarter and three full-backs.

1875 - Tries were used to decide results. If both teams scored the same number of goals or if no goals were kicked, the match was decided on the majority of tries.

1877 - Team sizes reduced from 20 to 15.

1883 - The first Home Nations Championship is run with England emerging as inaugural victors, winning all of their three games.

1886 - A numerical value was adopted by the RFU for tries and goals. Tries earned one point, conversions two and a goal from a mark, three.

1886 - The International Rugby Football Board is formed by Scotland, Ireland and Wales and in **1890** the IRFB draws up one international code of laws.

1895 - The great split: rugby league and rugby union become two separate sports.

1899 - Australia play their first Test match, against the touring side from Great Britain.

1991

1900 - Rugby is included in the Olympic Games, with gold won by France, although it was dropped from the Games after the 1924 event.

1905 - The first recorded schoolboy international takes place between England and Wales.

1908 - With France playing friendlies against the other home nations, the first Grand Slam is awarded, to Wales.

1910 - France join the Home Nations Championship so it becomes known as the Five Nations.

1995

1921 - South Africa visit Australia and New Zealand, for the first time, winning all three Tests in Australia.

1925 - The New Zealand side known as The Invincibles visit Europe, winning every one of their 32 games on tour.

1931 - The Bledisloe Cup is presented by the then-Governor General of New Zealand, Lord Bledisloe, for matches between New Zealand and Australia. The

The Policeman who stands in the way.

The iconic image of Mandela and Pienaar

split occurred in England. Rugby had always been a fiercely amateur sport, with its roots in the public schools of England, but it became clear the 'northern clubs' were being run on different lines. So in August 1895, 22 clubs broke away from the RFU to form the Northern Union and eventually the game we know today as rugby league began.

In the decades that followed, union rulers fought a number of battles with those who tried to end its status as an amateur sport, as they sought to allow players and coaches to be paid for the work they did.

This battle led to France being expelled from the Five Nations Championship in 1931 and due to its cessation during the Second World War they were not readmitted until 1947. That campaign against amateurism finally ended in 1995 when the then-chairman of the IRB, Vernon Pugh (below), declared the game of rugby union 'open' so players and coaches could be paid.

placed on an unstoppable path to professionalism by the advent of a World Cup for the sport. In the same year the first competitive leagues were established in England.

Professional rugby union quickly became an unmitigated success, even if the northern hemisphere unions were slower to adapt to the pace of the new structure than their cousins in the southern hemisphere.

It took until the fifth World Cup, in 2003, for a side from the north to win it, Clive Woodward's exceptional England side beating Australia in the final with an injury-time drop goal from Jonny Wilkinson (below).

The most powerful symbol of rugby in the modern era was created at the 1995 World Cup when the winning South African captain, Francois Pienaar, was presented with the Webb Ellis Cup by the country's president, Nelson Mandela, while Mandela was dressed in a replica of Pienaar's Springbok jersey, an image that typifies rugby union.

KEY RUGBY DATES

All Blacks win it first.

1933 - The Wallabies make their first tour to South Africa for a Test series, won by South Africa 3-1.

1939 - The tour of the 1939 Wallabies is cancelled when war is declared the day after the team arrive in England. After two weeks in England, the team returns home.

1948 - Australia are invited to join the International Rugby Football Board. This invitation gives impetus to the formation of an Australian Rugby Union. The drop goal is reduced from four points to three.

1949 - The inaugural meeting of the Australian Rugby Union is held on 25th November with 11 delegates from the six states.

1978 - New Zealand complete a Grand Slam of wins in the home nations, Australia following suit in 1984.

1981 - Mark, Gary and Glen Ella become the first three brothers to be chosen in the same Wallaby squad.

1987 - The inaugural Rugby World Cup is played in Australia and New Zealand. It is won by New Zealand who beat France in the final to lift the Webb Ellis Cup.

1991 - The second Rugby World Cup is held in the northern hemisphere with Australia defeating England 12-6 in the final at Twickenham.

1992 - The value of a try is increased from four to five points. The conversion stays at two points with the drop goal and penalty each worth three. South Africa play their first Test, against Australia, since the end of apartheid in allowed them to return to Test competition.

1995 - The third Rugby World Cup takes place in South Africa, drawing a worldwide TV audience of over one billion viewers. It is won by South Africa. International rugby union becomes professional at all levels. The southern hemisphere rugby countries of South Africa, New Zealand and Australia form SANZAR to run the Super 12 and Tri-Nations. The Heineken Cup is launched in Europe. Auckland Blues win the first Super 12 and Toulouse the first Heineken Cup.

1997 - The Bledisloe Cup is played at the Melbourne Cricket Ground, the first international rugby game played at the MCG, and draws a crowd of 83,000.

1998 - The first Women's World Cup is sanctioned by the IRB and won by New Zealand.

1999 - Wales hosts the fourth Rugby World Cup. Australia win for the second time, beating France in the final in Cardiff.

2000 - The Five Nations becomes Six when Italy join. They win their first game against Scotland.

2001 - Australia wins their first series ever against the British and Irish Lions.

2003 - The fifth World Cup is hosted by Australia. England win the trophy, playing Australia in the final at Telstra Stadium, Sydney.

2006 - The Super 12 competition expands into a Super 14 with the addition of the Western Force (Perth) and the Cheetahs from South Africa, rejecting either Argentina or a side from the Pacific Islands.

2007 - The sixth World Cup is hosted in France and won by South Africa, who beat England in the final 15-6. George Gregan retires as the most-capped (139 Tests) rugby player ever.

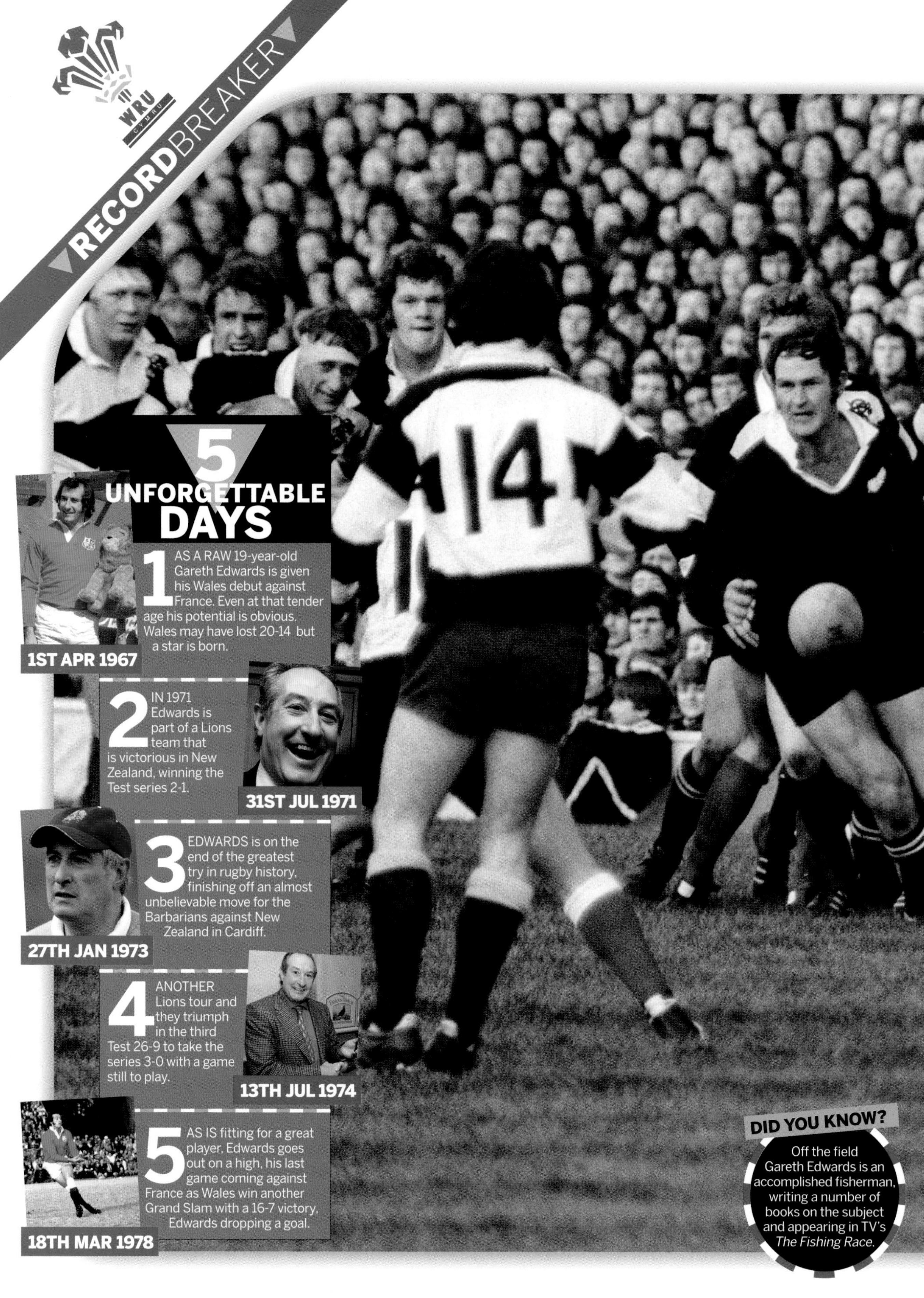

5 UNFORGETTABLE DAYS

1 AS A RAW 19-year-old Gareth Edwards is given his Wales debut against France. Even at that tender age his potential is obvious. Wales may have lost 20-14 but a star is born.

1ST APR 1967

2 IN 1971 Edwards is part of a Lions team that is victorious in New Zealand, winning the Test series 2-1.

31ST JUL 1971

3 EDWARDS is on the end of the greatest try in rugby history, finishing off an almost unbelievable move for the Barbarians against New Zealand in Cardiff.

27TH JAN 1973

4 ANOTHER Lions tour and they triumph in the third Test 26-9 to take the series 3-0 with a game still to play.

13TH JUL 1974

5 AS IS fitting for a great player, Edwards goes out on a high, his last game coming against France as Wales win another Grand Slam with a 16-7 victory, Edwards dropping a goal.

18TH MAR 1978

DID YOU KNOW?

Off the field Gareth Edwards is an accomplished fisherman, writing a number of books on the subject and appearing in TV's *The Fishing Race*.

GARETH EDWARDS

Edwards in a Lions shirt and (left) in the famous game for the Barbarians against New Zealand

After the 1974 trip Lions captain Willie John McBride described Edwards as 'the best scrum-half I have seen or am ever likely to see'.

REGARDED BY almost every commentator as the greatest player ever to come out of the Welsh nation, Edwards is considered by many as the best player ever to play the game of rugby union.

He was simply undroppable in his career with Wales and the British & Irish Lions. From the day he made his debut for Wales in 1967 until his last appearance, 11 years later, he was never left out of the team, and his Wales record of 53 consecutive Tests has still not been overtaken.

Awarded the CBE for his services to rugby in 2007, Edwards had the pace, vision and tactical genius to make many people think he could have been a star even in the modern era. An all-round sportsman, he won a sports scholarship to the prestigious Millfield School, making his Wales debut as a teenager.

During Edwards's career Wales enjoyed the greatest success in their history, lifting the Five Nations Championship seven times. On three of those occasions they were unbeaten, taking a Grand Slam.

For much of that time he formed an irresistible half-back partnership with the inspirational Barry John.

A fitness fanatic, who always had the attitude of a professional player, Edwards was Wales' youngest ever captain, skippering the team when aged just 20 and going on to lead the side a further 12 times.

Edwards didn't just make his name playing for Wales, his sensational skills being paraded ten times for the British & Irish Lions as they won the 1971 series in New Zealand and again in South Africa, in 1974.

After the 1974 trip Lions captain Willie John McBride described him as 'the best scrum-half I have seen or am ever likely to see'.

Edwards also scored perhaps rugby's most famous try when he finished off an incredible, length-of-the-field move for the Barbarians as they beat New Zealand in 1973.

In 2003 Edwards topped a poll in *Rugby World Magazine*, declaring him the greatest player of all time, and a statue has been erected of him in Cardiff.

Fact file

Full name: Gareth Owen Edwards
Date of birth: 12 July, 1947
Place of birth: Gwaun-Cae-Gurwen
School: Millfield
Position: Scrum-half
First cap: 1967 v France
Test caps: 53
Test points: 88

RECORDBREAKER

DAVID CAMPESE

'He has a special genius which shows an individual can still leave an indelible mark to treasure,' said Barry John.

ONE OF THE most flamboyant players ever to grace the rugby field, David Campese was the world-record holder for tries scored in Test matches for more than a decade, grabbing 64 in 101 games for Australia.

A World Cup winner in 1991, Campo, as he was universally known, was deadly with ball in hand, a maverick who wasn't even sure himself what he was going to do next, so pity the defenders who were asked to mark him.

He was at the heart of a golden generation for Australian rugby, first emerging on the world stage in 1984 when he helped the Wallabies to a Grand Slam of victories over England, Scotland, Ireland and Wales.

A thorn in New Zealand's side throughout his 14-year career, Campese knocked them out of the 1991 World Cup with a mesmerising performance in the semi-final, before going on to help the Wallabies lift the trophy with a win over England.

It was not all highs for Campo, who invented the goosestep move, as he is blamed for Australia losing the 1989 Lions tour. With the series tied, in the final game, Campese threw an outrageous pass, behind his own goal line, which Greg Martin failed to gather. Ieuan Evans pounced and delivered the series victory.

His outspoken views sometimes got him in trouble and in 2003 he was forced to parade through the streets of London carrying a banner (left) accepting England's World Cup win.

Fact file

Full name: David Ian Campese
Date of birth: 21 October, 1962
Place of birth: Queanbeyan, Australia
Nickname: Campo
Position: Wing
First cap: 1982 v New Zealand
Test caps: 101
Test tries: 64
Test points: 315

STAT ATTACK

David Campese's 64 Test tries was a world record established in 1996, until Japan's Daisuke Ohata scored his 65th try playing for Japan on 14 May 2006.

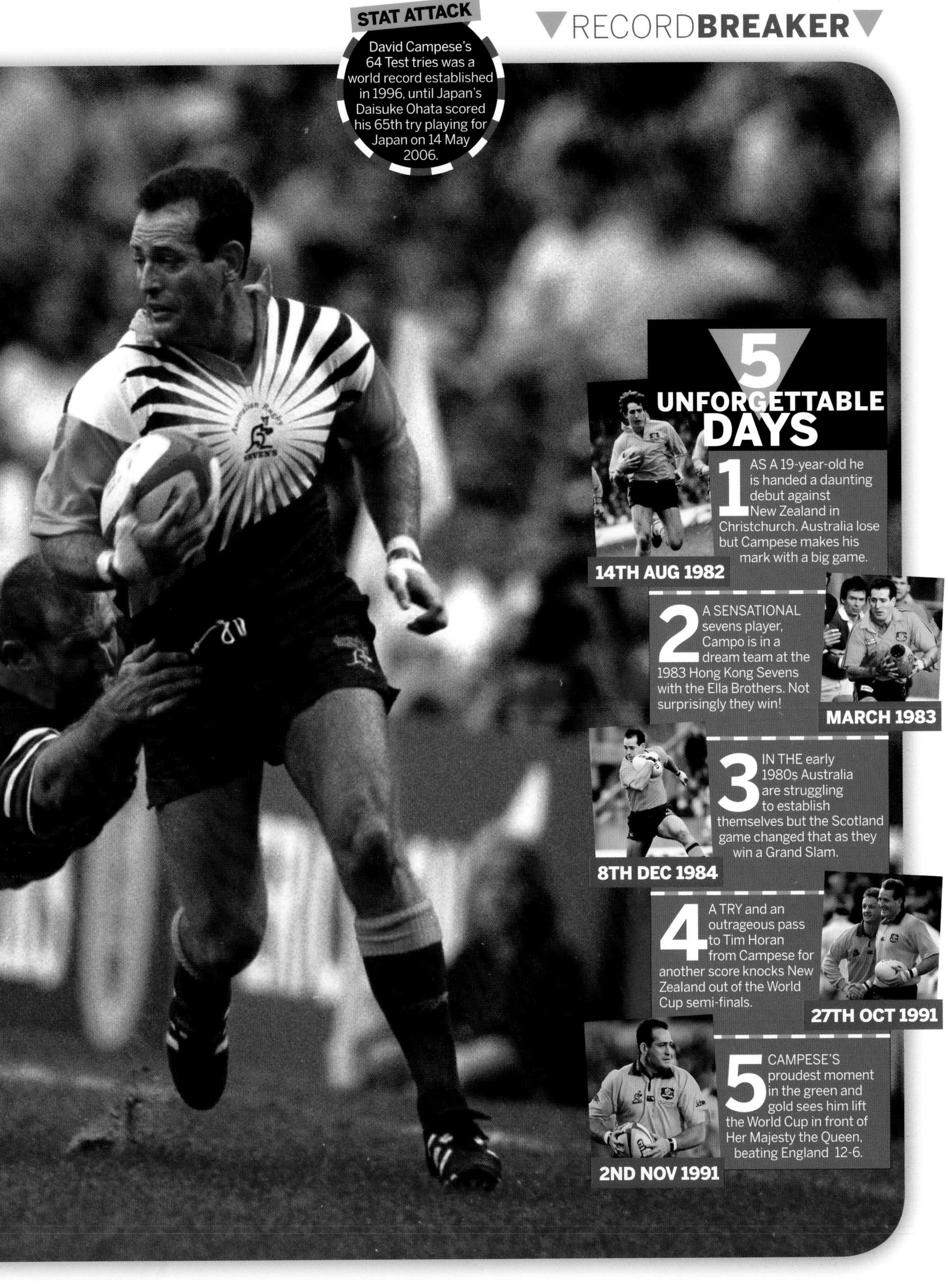

5 UNFORGETTABLE DAYS

14TH AUG 1982

1 AS A 19-year-old he is handed a daunting debut against New Zealand in Christchurch. Australia lose but Campese makes his mark with a big game.

MARCH 1983

2 A SENSATIONAL sevens player, Campo is in a dream team at the 1983 Hong Kong Sevens with the Ella Brothers. Not surprisingly they win!

8TH DEC 1984

3 IN THE early 1980s Australia are struggling to establish themselves but the Scotland game changed that as they win a Grand Slam.

27TH OCT 1991

4 A TRY and an outrageous pass to Tim Horan from Campese for another score knocks New Zealand out of the World Cup semi-finals.

2ND NOV 1991

5 CAMPESE'S proudest moment in the green and gold sees him lift the World Cup in front of Her Majesty the Queen, beating England 12-6.

NEW ZEALAND ALL BLACKS

RECORD BREAKER

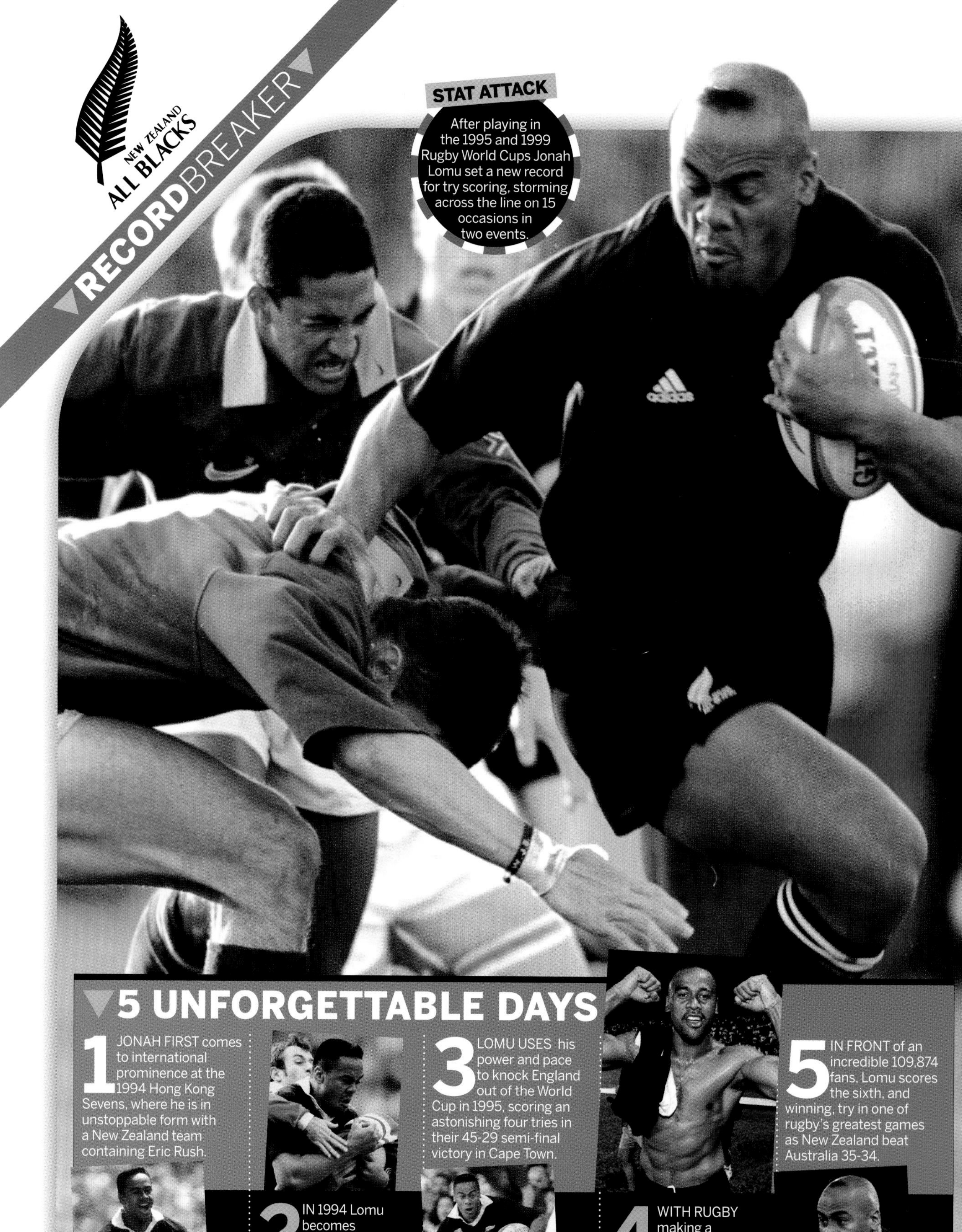

STAT ATTACK

After playing in the 1995 and 1999 Rugby World Cups Jonah Lomu set a new record for try scoring, storming across the line on 15 occasions in two events.

5 UNFORGETTABLE DAYS

1 JONAH FIRST comes to international prominence at the 1994 Hong Kong Sevens, where he is in unstoppable form with a New Zealand team containing Eric Rush.

MARCH 1994

2 IN 1994 Lomu becomes the youngest New Zealand international in history, playing in the 22-8 defeat by France, having just passed his 19th birthday.

26TH JUN 1994

3 LOMU USES his power and pace to knock England out of the World Cup in 1995, scoring an astonishing four tries in their 45-29 semi-final victory in Cape Town.

18TH JUN 1995

4 WITH RUGBY making a return to the Commonwealth Games, Lomu helps New Zealand to the gold medal in Malaysia as the other sides have no answer.

14TH SEP 1998

5 IN FRONT of an incredible 109,874 fans, Lomu scores the sixth, and winning, try in one of rugby's greatest games as New Zealand beat Australia 35-34.

19TH JUL 2000

JONAH LOMU

Fact file

Full name: Jonah Tali Lomu
Date of birth: 12 May, 1975
Place of birth: Auckland, New Zealand
Height: 6ft 5in (1.96m)
Weight: 18st 8lb (119kg)
School: Wesley College
Position: Wing
Test caps: 63
Test points: 185

RUGBY'S FIRST global superstar, Jonah Lomu became the most famous rugby player in the world as the game turned professional in 1995. A devastating runner, he trampled over players from every country, wreaking havoc in a stunning career that brought him 37 tries in 63 Tests.

England captain Will Carling called him a freak and you can understand why when you consider that at 6ft 5in he is as tall as many second-rows and at almost 19 stone is as heavy as some props. But despite his height and weight he ran like the wind and demolished England at the 1995 World Cup. Carling's England arrived in South Africa as Grand Slam champions and one of the favourites – that was until Lomu shattered their dreams in an unforgettable performance when he scored four tries as England were steamrollered 45-29.

And unfortunately for England he hadn't finished with them yet, scoring a try from halfway to beat them in the 1999 World Cup, a defeat that effectively knocked them out, as it forced them into a quarter-final play-off.

Lomu's abilities were obvious from a young age and in 1994 at 19 years and 45 days, he became the youngest All Black Test player ever, against France, after making a name for himself with a devastating performance at the Hong Kong Sevens that year.

Kris Babicci, the Chief Executive of Standard Chartered Bank, explained best the effect Lomu had: 'During the 1990s, Lomu was responsible for changing rugby. He was the face of rugby and in the process became the sport's first true superstar.'

Lomu's incredible career was achieved despite him suffering from a debilitating kidney disease for much of his adult life. He had a transplant in 2004 and made a brave attempt to get back to his best, still playing club rugby but failing to make the All Blacks team again.

On the burst in the 1999 World Cup against France

'Lomu was responsible for changing rugby. He was the face of rugby and in the process became the sport's first true superstar.'

Hard to stop, Jonah was a legend

STAT ATTACK

South Africa's 2007 World Cup-winning captain John Smit has led his country more times (48 by the end of 2007) than any other player in their history.

FIVE GREAT PLAYERS

1. FRANCOIS PIENAAR: The iconic captain who united a nation as well as a rugby team in 1995 to deliver the World Cup at the first attempt. A true rugby legend who transcended the game.

2. FRIK DU PREEZ: A giant lock who ruled the lineout in the 1950s. He was an all-round lock who could run with the ball, could kick and even drop goal.

3. JOOST VAN DER WESTHUIZEN: One of the greatest scrum-halves in the history of the game, he retired in 2003 but by the end of 2007 his record of 38 tries still hadn't been overtaken by any other South African.

4. ERROL TOBIAS: He became the first black man to play for South Africa, making his debut in 1981 against Ireland.

5. PAUL ROOS: A rugby pioneer, Roos took the first South African team overseas in 1906 when they played 29 games in Britain.

GROUNDS

SOUTH AFRICA try to keep their many millions of fans happy by rotating their Test matches almost across the length and breadth of the country, giving the option of playing at sea level or at altitude where the air is thinner and the rugby tougher.

Their biggest stadium is the vast Ellis Park in Johannesburg, where they won the 1995 World Cup, but they use Pretoria's Loftus Versfeld, Newlands in Cape Town, the ABSA Stadium in Durban, and the EPRFU Stadium in Port Elizabeth, along with the Vodacom Park in Bloemfontein, where they played their first home Test as world champions, against Wales in June 2008. Port Elizabeth's St George's Park Cricket Ground hosted the first Test in 1891.

SOUTH AFRICA

ONE OF two countries alongside Australia to have won the World Cup twice, South Africa lifted the Webb Ellis Cup on home soil in 1995 and again when the World Cup tournament came to France in 2007.

The Springboks arrived at the sixth World Cup with a formidable side led by Jake White, a coach who had an unbreakable bond with his captain, John Smit and they were, in the eyes of almost every observer, deserved winners against England in the final.

The victory ended a few years in the wilderness for the Springboks as they failed to kick on from their success at the 1995 event.

Everything changed in South African sport in the 1970s when all sporting contact with the Republic was suspended because of their abhorrent apartheid political regime that separated blacks and whites. This sporting ban meant that South Africa missed the first two World Cups in 1987 and 1991, but after apartheid collapsed soon after there was only one place to stage the 1995: South Africa. The Rainbow Nation responded with a sensational tournament that ended with Springboks captain Francois Pienaar receiving the cup from Nelson Mandela, then the country's president, after they beat New Zealand in the final 15-12, at Ellis Park, Johannesburg.

Captained by rugby legend Francois Pienaar, the side broke up after the tournament but they still managed to equal New Zealand's record for consecutive Test wins (of 17) between 1997 and 1998.

After Jake White's departure following the 2007 World Cup win, the South Africans appointed their first black coach, Peter de Villiers, to the helm as they try to defend their title and prepare the nation for a British & Irish Lions tour in 2009.

DID YOU KNOW?
South Africa full-back Percy Montgomery holds the country's record for most points scored (873) and caps won (94) after the 2007 World Cup.

Quick stats

TEAM COLOURS: Green and Gold
NICKNAME: Springboks
HONOURS: World Cup winners (1995, 2007); Tri-Nations champions (1998, 2004)
ADDRESS: 5th Floor, Boundary Road, PO Box 99, Newlands 7725, Cape Town, South Africa
www.sarugby.co.za

Everything changed for South African sport in the 1970s...but they returned to international competition in victory.

BEST DAY

BACK IN international competition for three years, no one could have written a better script for South African rugby than playing the World Cup on their own soil. And the Boy's Own story was completed at Ellis Park when the Springboks beat New Zealand 15-12 (right).

24TH JUNE 1995

WORST DAY

EIGHT YEARS after winning the World Cup, South African rugby was in disarray. Divisions in the squad came out in the horrendous 29-9 defeat they suffered to New Zealand in the World Cup quarter-final (right). They had already lost to England and bowed out meekly.

8TH NOV 2003

FIRST TEST MATCH

IT WAS the British & Irish Lions who gave South Africa their first taste of international rugby, 15 years after the game first surfaced in the country. Back in 1891 the Springboks kicked off with a 4-0 victory and they have enjoyed some epic battles with the tourists since.

30TH JUL 1891

FRANCE

IT TOOK FRANCE until 1968 to win their first Grand Slam, to be finally confirmed as the best side in Europe, but they quickly made up for lost time, becoming the championship's most consistent team in following decades.

Only joining the newly-named Five Nations Championship in 1910, the French had a tempestuous introduction to international rugby, failing to beat England until 1927 and then finding themselves expelled from the championship in 1932 (until 1947) amid allegations of professionalism in the French leagues.

France did, however, support the rugby competitions at the Olympics, winning gold in 1900 and two silvers in the 1920s.

As with so many countries, a special group of players changed everything about French rugby, emerging in the 1950s with an uncompromising brand of play coupled with the flair which has captivated fans from around the globe. This new era culminated in France's first Five Nations title in 1959, with players like Jean Prat, André Boniface and Michael Crauste at its core.

The great deeds of the 1950s and 1960s were carried into the next two decades by another golden generation, who had the flair and panache to score some of the most wonderful tries the game has seen.

France have made the knockout stages of every World Cup but never collected the trophy, coming closest when runners-up in 1987 and 1999.

Quick stats

TEAM COLOURS: Blue and white
NICKNAME: Les Bleus
HONOURS: World Cup runners-up (1987, 1999), Grand Slams (8): 1968, 1977, 1981, 1987, 1997, 1998, 2002, 2004
ADDRESS: Fédération Française de rugby, 9 Rue de Liège, Paris 75009

www.ffr.com

DID YOU KNOW?

When the Five Nations was turned into Six by Italy's inclusion in 2000, France were the first side to complete a Grand Slam, winning it in 2002.

FIVE GREAT PLAYERS

1. PHILIPPE SELLA: The first Frenchman to win 100 Test caps, Philippe Sella, was a master craftsman in the centre.

2. SERGE BLANCO: The artisan of European rugby in the 1980s, Blanco summed up everything good about French rugby: flair, panache and the skill to light up a game.

3. JEAN PRAT: Prat was one of the catalysts for the French revival after the war. He won 51 caps in a 10-year Test career and captained them to their first wins over Wales and the All Blacks.

4. JEAN-PIERRE RIVES: The blond bombshell lit up the action in the 1970s and 80s. A fearsome openside respected everywhere.

5. RAPHAËL IBAÑEZ: The most capped hooker in the world, Ibañez was a warrior who led the team with courage.

GROUNDS

WITHOUT A national stadium to call their own, the French rugby team has played up and down the country. During the early years France played internationals at venues such as Parc des Princes and the Stade Olympique de Colombes, both in Paris.

But when the 80,000-capacity Stade de France was opened in 1998 for the Football World Cup, it was also adopted as the new home for French rugby. France has continued its tradition of playing games all over the country, regularly playing an autumn international in the smaller Stade Vélodrome in Marseilles and in recent years games have been staged at Stade Gerland, Lyon, Stade de la Beaujoire, Nantes and Stadium de Toulouse, Toulouse.

Frenchmen had the flair and panache to score some of the most wonderful tries the game of rugby has ever seen.

FRANCE

STAT ATTACK

Fabien Pelous became France's most-capped player in 2007, ending with 118. He also set a new record (of 42) for the times he captained his country.

▼BEST DAY

IN THE decades after the Second World War, rugby in France grew at a pace, culminating in a famous victory on Bastille Day, 1979, when they beat the All Blacks in New Zealand for the first time, winning 24-19 at Eden Park in Auckland, a huge step forward for the team.

14TH JUL 1979

Daniel Dubroca, a key part of the 1979 side

▼WORST DAY

BEFORE MAKING the final of the 1999 World Cup, France struggled a little, culminating in a terrible 1999 Five Nations season, when they picked up the wooden spoon by finishing last, their worst result (right) when they lost at home 36-22 to Scotland as the Scots took the title.

10TH APR 1999

▼FIRST TEST MATCH

THE NEW Zealand All Blacks kicked off the history of Test rugby in France in 1906, inflicting a 38-8 defeat. The Test match, in Paris, came six years after France competed in the Olympics and soon led to them playing the European nations on a regular basis.

1ST JAN 1906

STAT ATTACK

England's Jonny Wilkinson holds the world record for most drop goals in Test matches, kicking his 29th in the 2008 win over France in Paris.

▼FIVE GREAT PLAYERS

1. MARTIN JOHNSON: Arguably the greatest player ever to wear an England jersey. He led the country to their World Cup win in 2003 and won 84 caps in a 10-year international career, while leading the famous Leicester club.

2. RORY UNDERWOOD: The flyer from Leicester terrorised defences for 12 seasons in the 1980s and 1990s scoring 49 tries, more than any Englishman in the history of the game.

3. JONNY WILKINSON: No rugby player has scored more points in Test matches than Wilkinson, the man who delivered the crucial extra-time drop goal to beat Australia and win the World Cup in 2003.

4. JASON LEONARD: The first Englishman to win 100 Test caps, he was England's rock of ages in the front row.

5. WILL CARLING: Led England into a period of great success in the 1980s and 1990s and captained his country a world-record 59 times over eight years.

▼GROUNDS

TWICKENHAM IS the only ground used by the modern-day rugby union team although it wasn't always the case, as England have played in a number of different home stadiums.

Blackheath, The Oval, Manchester, Leicester, Dewsbury, Bristol, Richmond and Leeds all served the England team before Twickenham saw its first action in 1911 after being converted from a cabbage patch and being bought by RFU commitee man Billy Williams in 1907 for £5,572 12s and 6d.

After the game turned professional in 1995 England did play New Zealand at Old Trafford, Manchester, and used the McAlpine Stadium in Huddersfield, when they were forced to play Holland and Italy to qualify for the 1999 World Cup.

ENGLAND

THE FIRST European side to win the World Cup, in 2003, success was a long time coming for England, the biggest rugby nation in the world. Even if William Webb Ellis didn't pick up the ball and run with it as the myth would have us believe, England is still the spiritual home for the game of rugby and Rugby School in Warwickshire its birthplace.

As founders of the game, England played the first Test match back in 1871, when they lost to Scotland in Edinburgh in front of 4,000 people.

England are part of the annual Six Nations Championship, a tournament they have won 23 times. They have completed a clean sweep of wins (Grand Slam) 12 times, more than any other side.

England were a dominant force in the early years of rugby in the British Isles, winning Grand Slams in 1913 and 1914 after France joined the championship to make it the Five Nations.

DID YOU KNOW?
When the redevelopment of the home of English rugby, Twickenham, was completed in 2007 the grand old stadium could hold 82,000 supporters.

They fared badly in their clashes with the southern hemisphere powerhouses of South Africa, New Zealand and Australia until the game turned professional in 1995, when the country with the largest number of adult players in the world started to assert their position.

In 2002 England beat South Africa, New Zealand and Australia in the space of 14 days, laying the foundation for their World Cup win in 2003. Four years later they were runners-up to South Africa in the World Cup.

An appearance in the 1991 final (which was held at England's home of Twickenham) was their best effort up to that time, although they have competed in all six World Cups.

Their biggest win in Test matches was the 134-0 victory over Romania in 2001, although they again passed the 100-point mark against Uruguay at the 2003 World Cup.

England dominated in the early years of rugby in the British Isles…and became the first European side to win the Rugby World Cup.

Quick stats

TEAM COLOURS: White with red trim
NICKNAME: None
HONOURS: World Cup winners (2003); Grand Slams (12): 1913, 1914, 1921, 1923, 1924, 1928, 1957, 1980, 1991, 1992, 1995, 2003
ADDRESS: Rugby House, Rugby Road, Twickenham, England, TW1 1DS.
www.rfu.com

▼BEST DAY

THERE IS only one candidate for England's best day, the time when they lifted the World Cup, by beating Australia 20-17 in Sydney. Coach Clive Woodward was later knighted and some 750,000 lined the streets of London to welcome the side on their return home.

22ND NOV 2003

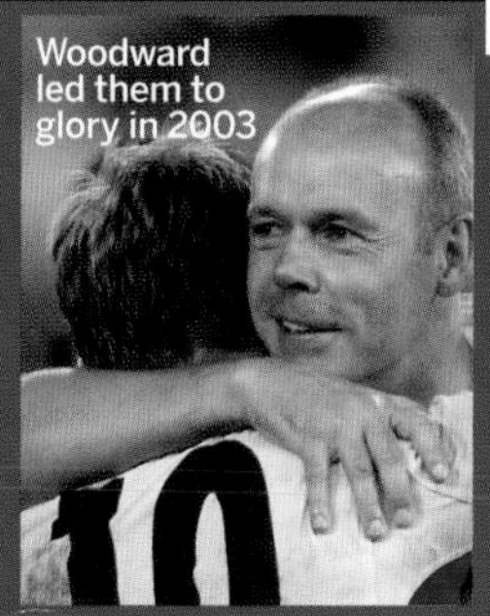

Woodward led them to glory in 2003

▼WORST DAY

IN 1998 England went on an ill-fated tour to the southern hemisphere and, although it was Jonny Wilkinson's first start in an England shirt, they were hammered 76-0 by Australia. They went from Australia to lose in New Zealand and South Africa in the *Tour from Hell.*

6TH JUNE 1998

There wasn't much to take from the 76-0 hammering

▼FIRST TEST MATCH

ENGLAND WERE privileged enough to play in rugby union's first-ever Test match, back in 1871 when the game was 20-a-side! The game was played against Scotland in Edinburgh and the Scots won by one goal (converted try) and one try to the one try scored by England.

27TH MAR 1871

COUNTRIES

NEW ZEALAND

ANOTHER COUNTRY where rugby is the national sport, New Zealanders eat, breathe, and live rugby like no other place on the planet.

Their rugby has stood like a colossus over the rugby world since New South Wales became the first side to tour New Zealand in 1882.

Two early teams in particular, the Originals of 1905-06 and the Invincibles of 1924-25, shaped many parts of the game of rugby union we see today, setting new standards with incredible records.

The All Blacks' domination has ensured that, remarkably, they have a winning record against every other rugby nation, with their closest and fiercest rivals over the decades being South Africa.

The All Blacks of the mid- to late-1960s also established a world record (later equalled by South Africa) by winning 17 consecutive Test matches.

It was therefore fitting that New Zealand managed to win the first World Cup, staged in New Zealand and Australia in 1987, as they cut a swathe through the rest of the rugby world. They won the final 29-9, against France, their smallest winning margin in the tournament.

But perhaps more surprising than this first victory is the fact that they haven't managed to win the Webb Ellis Cup again. If someone had said in 1987 the All Blacks wouldn't win the World Cup for at least another 24 years they would have been considered mad!

But they managed to blow successive tournaments, while beating every nation in between the World Cups. This run culminated in their loss to France at the 2007 World Cup, a result that stunned everyone in the rugby world.

Since its inception in 1996 New Zealand have dominated the Tri-Nations Championship, held every year to determine the best side in the southern hemisphere. In the first ten years of the Tri-Nations, the Kiwis won the competition seven times, completing a clean sweep three times in 1996, 1997 and 2003.

The All Blacks have been a sensational rugby side over the years, setting world records at every turn and winning the first World Cup.

Quick stats

TEAM COLOURS: Black
NICKNAME: All Blacks
HONOURS: World Cup winners (1987); Tri-Nations champions (1996, 1997, 1999, 2002, 2003, 2005, 2006, 2007)
ADDRESS: New Zealand RU,1 Hinemoa St, Harbour Quays Wellington PO Box 2172.
www.allblacks.com

BEST DAY

THERE WAS a certain inevitability about New Zealand's sole World Cup win in 1987 as they demolished every side they played, including a 49-6 win over Wales in the semi-finals. France were despatched 29-9 at Eden Park as David Kirk (right) lifted the cup.

20TH JUN 1987

WORST DAY

NEW ZEALAND went into the 2007 World Cup as the hottest favourites in the history of the competition. But their hopes came crashing down in Cardiff in the quarter-finals (right) when they lost 20-18 to France, after leading 13-0, arguably the biggest shock in World Cup history.

6TH OCT 2007

FIRST TEST MATCH

A NUMBER of All Blacks sides played nationally recognised games at the end of the 19th century but the first New Zealand Test match came in 1903 when they beat Australia in Sydney 22-3, on one of their tours. Four years later in Australia they were unbeaten in three Tests.

15TH AUG 1903

DID YOU KNOW?

The All Blacks are famous for performing a war dance or challenge before every game they play called. It's called the Haka, a crucial part of the Maori culture.

GROUNDS

WITHOUT A national ground of their own New Zealand play their rugby union Tests up and down the country, keeping a rugby-hungry public on both islands, in the Land of the Long White Cloud, happy.

Auckland's Eden Park, which will host both World Cup semi-finals and the final in 2011, is the biggest and most famous, hosting every high-profile side that has visited New Zealand, and the cup final in 1987.

The first Test match against New Zealand's biggest rivals, South Africa, was staged in 1921 in Dunedin, a city with strong Scottish connections. Australia played their first game there in 1905, but when the 2005 Lions toured the country the Test matches were hosted in the cities of Christchurch, Wellington and Auckland.

FIVE GREAT PLAYERS

1. GEORGE NEPIA: A sensational full-back from the Invincibles side of 1924-25, the only one to play in all 32 matches, while scoring 77 points.

2. COLIN MEADS: Known through the rugby world as Pinetree, Meads strode over New Zealand rugby like a colossus, fittingly being named Player of the Century at the NZRFU Awards dinner in 1999.

3. SEAN FITZPATRICK: A World Cup winner in 1987, Fitzy captained his country a record 51 times, playing in an amazing world-record 63 consecutive Tests.

4. JONAH LOMU: Rugby's first global superstar, Lomu made a huge impact on the game in the mid-1990s, using his immense pace and power to smash defences.

5. SIR BRIAN LOCHORE: Another elder statesman who made his mark in the 1960s and early 1970s.

SCOTLAND

Scotland staged the first Test match, back in 1871, and have enjoyed an impressive history since then, winning the Calcutta Cup again in 2008.

SCOTLAND CAN rival England's claim to be the historical home of rugby union. Not only did they play in the first Test match against the English but they also hosted it, at their Raeburn Place ground in Edinburgh, and won it into the bargain. Along with playing the first Test match, the Scots claim the oldest continual rugby fixture, which was first played in 1858 between Merchiston Castle School and the former pupils of the Edinburgh Academy.

And Scotland is, of course, the birthplace of the shortened version of rugby, sevens, initially conceived by Ned Haig, a butcher from Melrose, as a fundraising event for his local club in 1883. Scotland's heritage in sevens made it the obvious place to host the first World Cup Sevens, in 1993, which England won by beating Australia.

The 1871 win over England didn't lead to domination for the Scots in the Five Nations and they had to wait until the 1920s for their first Grand Slam. That was a 1925 clean sweep, underpinned by one of the most prolific try scorers in the history of the competition, Ian Smith, who crossed the line eight times in the championship campaign, a record that still stands today.

In 1925, the year when Murrayfield was opened, the Scots clinched the Grand Slam with a 14-11 victory over England in front of 70,000 fans at their new home.

Once the game turned professional in 1995, Scotland restructured their club game, pouring all their resources into regional teams, which had many guises in the first decade. But by the time the Scots won the Calcutta Cup (a trophy on offer every time Scotland play England) in 2008, 15-9, there were just two, Edinburgh and Glasgow, providing the bulk of the players to the national side.

DID YOU KNOW?
Scotland's most prolific Championship season came in 1999 when they scored 120 points, winning the title on the final day when Wales beat England.

Quick stats

TEAM COLOURS: Dark blue and white
HONOURS: Grand Slams (3): 1925, 1984 and 1990
ADDRESS: Scottish Rugby
Murrayfield, Edinburgh
EH12 5PJ. Tel: 0131 346 5000
www.scottishrugby.org

BEST DAY

SCOTLAND ARRIVED at their Grand Slam decider with England in 1990, as underdogs. With the Calcutta Cup Championship, the Triple Crown and Grand Slam all on the table, Scotland triumphed 13-7, a try from Tony Stanger giving the Scots the crucial edge.

17TH MAR 1990

Captain David Sole leads out the team for the 1990 game

WORST DAY

IF THE 1990 Grand Slam was magnificent, disappointment arrived a year later when the Scots were one step from a World Cup final, only to see it snatched away by England, who won 9-6, Gavin Hastings missing a straightforward kick when the scores were tied 6-6.

26TH OCT 1991

Dejection for Gavin Hastings in 1991

FIRST TEST MATCH

NOT ONLY Scotland's first Test match but the world's first, when England arrived in Edinburgh to kick off international competition in this new sport. The game was played at Raeburn Place, on the cricket field of the Edinburgh Academy. Scotland ran out winners by a goal and a try to a goal.

27TH MAR 1871

STAT ATTACK

Scotland have hit treble figures in a Test match once, chalking up a round 100 points against the Japanese in 2004, in Perth, scoring a massive 15 tries.

FIVE GREAT PLAYERS

1. GAVIN HASTINGS: The country's leading points scorer delivered on many occasions for the Scots, making him one player they couldn't do without in the 1980s and 1990s.

2. SCOTT HASTINGS: Big Gav's brother took his Scottish appearance record, ending with 65 Tests to his name.

3. IAN SMITH: Eight tries in the 1925 Five Nations season as Scotland won a Grand Slam makes him a legend north of the border.

4. GREGOR TOWNSEND: A hero for Scotland and the Lions, he ended his career with more caps than any other Scot. Townsend was one of the most talented playmakers in Europe.

5. CHRIS PATERSON: A dead-eyed goalkicker who scored his 29th kick from 29 attempts to win the Calcutta Cup match in 2008. Shunted around the backline by a succession of coaches, he's near the top of the tree when it comes to points scored and tries.

GROUNDS

THE FIRST nine international matches in Scotland were all played on cricket fields. Following the first at the Edinburgh Academy, the second was played at Hamilton Crescent, Glasgow, the home of West of Scotland CCA. Old Hampden Park, Glasgow, for the 1896 match v England was the new home, while in 1897, the match v Ireland was played at Powderhall Stadium, Edinburgh.

Eventually, in 1897, the union purchased ground at Inverleith, Edinburgh, for the sum of £3,800. But when it was appreciated some years later that it couldn't cope with the demands of international rugby, the magnificent Murrayfield, where Scotland play today, was opened in 1925.

▼COUNTRIES▼

ITALY

ONE OF the new-age rugby countries, Italy joined the Championship in 2000, changing it from the Five to Six Nations and bringing a breath of fresh air to the oldest annual rugby tournament in the world.

Italy made a remarkable start to life in the Six Nations. Written off by many they won their first match, against Scotland, and quickly became a powerful force.

Their impact culminated in a sustained challenge in 2007 when they won two games in a Six Nations season for the first time, beating Scotland and Wales.

Italy are one of the fastest developing rugby teams in the world, capable of upsets, and they are becoming formidable foes in their home city.

The Italian rugby fans have certainly backed their rugby team, filling the 48,000-capacity Stadium Flaminio in Rome, expanded for the visit of England in 2008, and giving them a heroes' welcome when they returned to Rome from their exploits overseas in 2007.

The Italians have, so far, been unable to transfer the success they have attained in the Six Nations into their performances in the World Cup, although managing to draw New Zealand in the pool stages in 2003 and 2007 hasn't helped them progress in the tournament!

Italy have failed to make the quarter-finals once, their best World Cup campaign coming in 2003 when they at least picked up two wins, against Canada and Tonga, but lost out to Wales.

The lack of Italian-born players in their domestic championship has held Italy back a little and, as they move towards their second decade in the Six Nations, it is a situation that needs to be addressed if they are to progress.

The Italians have had a succession of overseas coaches and in 2007, after the World Cup, the former Springboks coach Nick Mallett took the helm from Frenchman Pierre Berbizier.

DID YOU KNOW?
At the 2007 World Cup one of their most treasured sons, Alessandro Troncon, became the first Italian to win 100 caps, joining an elite club.

Quick stats

TEAM COLOURS: Blue and white
NICKNAME: Azzurri
HONOURS: None
ADDRESS: Federazione Italiana Rugby, Via L. Franchetti 2 00194 Rome, Italy

www.federugby.it

▼BEST DAY

YOU COULDN'T have dreamt up a better Six Nations kick-off for Italy than their win in 2000 against Scotland, in Rome 34-20 (right). They had been knocking on the door of the old Five Nations and finally got let in, justifying their inclusion immediately by beating the Scots.

5TH FEB 2000

▼WORST DAY

SO MUCH was expected of Italy at the 2003 World Cup and a trip to the last eight for the first time would have ensured a big breakthrough for the Azzurri. But their playing resources were stretched by an unfriendly schedule and they went down 27-15 to the Welsh (right).

25TH OCT 2003

▼FIRST TEST MATCH

FRANCE AND Italy have always had strong links and it was the French who gave the Azzurri their first taste of a top-flight Test match in 1937, when the French were banned from the Five Nations Championship due to allegations over professionalism. Italy lost their first game 43-5.

17TH OCT 1978

STAT ATTACK

Diego Dominguez became the first Italian to score 900 Test points, ending his career with 1,010, although 27 of those were when he was playing for Argentina.

▼GROUNDS

DESPITE MANY attempts to persuade Italy to take some of their big games around the country, they have settled, certainly in the Six Nations, on playing at Rome's magnificent Stadio Flaminio, which was expanded in 2008 to hold 48,000 fans.

With only one side under a roof, it may not be the most comfortable venue in world rugby, but it has the character to make it a stadium that fans want to go back to again and again.

Built in 1957, it is also the home to the soccer team, AS Cisco Roma.

In their early years as Italy were establishing themselves as a world force, they played France in Padua, Naples, Parma and Brescia, while in 2001 the Springboks were hosted in Genoa and the 1995 All Blacks in Bologna.

▼FIVE GREAT PLAYERS

1. ALESSANDRO TRONCON: The first Italian to win 100 caps, the combative scrum-half made his debut in 1994, winning his final cap at the 2007 World Cup.

2. DIEGO DOMINGUEZ: A goalkicker extraordinaire, only Neil Jenkins and Jonny Wilkinson have surpassed him in Tests.

3. MASSIMO GIOVANELLI: The heartbeat of the Italian side that won a place in the Six Nations. Fearsome in defence, he never took a backward step.

4. ANDRE LO CICERO: The prop from Sicily, who plays for French club Metro-Racing Paris, has made a huge impact since his debut in 2000. Missed just one Six Nations game from the 2004 season to 2008.

5. SERGIO PARISSE: The destructive No 8 from Stade Francais was coach Nick Mallett's first selection as captain when he took over in 2008. A great leader, and one who could take Italy forward in the future.

STAT ATTACK

Ireland, unlike many other leading nations, have never scored 100 points in a Test match, the most being the 83 they ran past USA on a tour in 2000.

FIVE GREAT PLAYERS

1. JACKIE KYLE: The artisan of the 1948 Grand Slam side, Kyle was the magician pulling the strings in their formidable back-line.

2. WILLIE JOHN MCBRIDE: One of the foremost leaders of men to play rugby union. He may have made his name in the red of the Lions but still won 63 Irish caps in a 14-season career.

3. KEITH WOOD: The face of Irish rugby for many years, the hooker led his country with distinction in what was a record 36 Tests.

4. BRIAN O'DRISCOLL: O'Driscoll took Keith Wood's record, captaining Ireland more times than anyone in the history of the game. A sensational, game-breaking runner, O'Driscoll became the first back to play for Ireland 80 times.

5. RONAN O'GARA: The first Irishman to score more than 800 points for his country, O'Gara is a great leader and master tactician. A Munsterman who won two Heineken Cups, he kicked Ireland to many victories.

GROUNDS

ONE OF rugby's most loved grounds, Lansdowne Road, has been host to Ireland for the majority of time since they kicked-off international rugby in 1875, although their first home game, against England, was staged at Leinster Cricket Club in Rathmines.

After those early days they stayed primarily in Dublin, but played England in Cork in 1905, and in Belfast, before playing a number of Tests at Ravenhill, Limerick hosting Wales in 1898 to make their Test debut.

The redevelopment of Lansdowne Road saw the Irish move, in 2007, into a temporary home at the 82,500-capacity Croke Park, which was so long exclusively the home of Gaelic football and hurling.

IRELAND

THE IRISH rugby team is unique in sporting terms as it represents both Eire and Northern Ireland, uniting two communities through sport and the love of a great game.

The Irish, whose team is based on players from the four provinces of Munster, Ulster, Connacht and Leinster, have put in a succession of strong performances in the Five and Six Nations but have the worst record of any Five Nations side, in terms of Grand Slams, winning just one in their history, in 1948. However, they have taken the title outright 10 times, and in 2007 came within a couple of minutes of winning every game, France taking the crown with a late try at Croke Park, Dublin.

Despite those failures to clinch a clean sweep for more than 60 years, Ireland have produced some of the championship's biggest characters, players like Keith Wood, Brian O'Driscoll and Willie John McBride, who have left an indelible mark on the European rugby scene.

DID YOU KNOW?
When Ireland play home matches they sing two anthems, the national anthem of the Republic of Ireland and the specially written Ireland's Call.

Outside of the Five and Six Nations, Ireland have been European's biggest underachievers in the World Cup, being the only one of the four home nations not to make at least a semi.

This series of poor performances in pursuit of the Webb Ellis Cup culminated in an embarrassing pool-stage exit in 2007, when many pundits were tipping them, under Eddie O'Sullivan, for a place in the last four.

They were in a tough group with Argentina and France in 2007 but disappointing performances against both Namibia and Georgia left them having to beat Argentina and score four tries in the final game. They achieved neither and went home.

Quick stats

TEAM COLOURS: Green and white
HONOURS: Grand Slam (1) in 1948
ADDRESS: 10-12 Lansdowne Road, Dublin 4, Ireland
Tel: 00353 1 6473800
Tickets: ticketqueries@Irishrugby.ie
www.IrishRugby.ie

Ireland have won just one Grand Slam, back in 1948, although they have managed to win the championship title outright 10 times.

BEST DAY

BELFAST'S RAVENHILL Ground was the scene of Ireland's greatest day as they clinched their one and only Grand Slam in 1948 with a hard-fought 6-3 win over Wales. London Irish's John Daly, the loosehead prop, scored the decisive try, *The Irish Independent* called him 'the green tornado'.

13TH MAR 1948

WORST DAY

IRELAND'S LOWEST ebb probably came in the 2007 World Cup when they squeezed past lowly Georgia in a pool match, 14-10, with tries from Girvan Dempsey (left) and Rory Best (right) in Bordeaux. The result set the tone for an awful campaign for the Irish.

15TH SEPT 2007

FIRST TEST MATCH

ENGLAND WERE Ireland's first opponents back in 1875 when the Irish made the trip to London to play the English at The Oval. As England had been playing Test rugby since 1871 it wasn't surprising that England emerged winners by one goal, one drop goal and a try to nil.

15TH FEB 1875

WALES

Wales enjoyed their greatest success in the 1970s when an incredibly talented group of players led the nation to a series of major successes.

ONE OF THE few countries in the world where rugby is the national sport, the game has always meant more to Welshmen that practically any other nation on earth.

Unlike in England where the game was the almost exclusive domain of the public schools in the early years, rugby union caught fire in working-class areas of Wales.

A victory over the Original All Blacks in 1905 (3-0) ensured Wales' place in the high echelons of the early rugby world, Grand Slams following this great start to life on the international stage. In 1908 they followed it up with a win over Australia, 9-6.

Wales enjoyed their greatest success in the 1970s when an incredibly talented group of players led the nation to a series of Grand Slams, Triple Crowns and Five Nations titles as the rugby world sat back and marvelled at players like Gareth Edwards, Mervyn Davies, Barry John, JJ Williams, John Dawes, JPR Williams, Gerald Davies and the famous Pontypool front row of Graham Price, Charlie Faulkner and Bobby Windsor.

Wales lost their way in the 1980s and 1990s, as they failed to adapt to the new challenges professionalism brought to the sport.

A semi-final berth in the first World Cup, in 1987, was followed by a succession of failures, culminating in their inability to qualify for the quarter-finals in 2003 and 2007, the latest campaign ending when they lost to Fiji.

These two disappointing campaigns were punctuated by a spectacular Grand Slam in 2005.

In 2008 Wales appointed a new coaching team in New Zealander Warren Gatland, Englishman Shaun Edwards and Welshman Rob Howley, and they had an instant impact delivering a Six Nations Grand Slam in their first season.

DID YOU KNOW?
Wales have only scored 100 points once in their history as they put 102 past Portugal in 1994, qualifying for the World Cup a year later.

Quick stats

TEAM COLOURS: Red and White
NICKNAME: Dragons
HONOURS: Grand Slam (10): 1908, 1909, 1911, 1950, 1952, 1971, 1976, 1978, 2005, 2008
ADDRESS: Welsh Rugby Union, St Mary's Street, Cardiff, Wales, CF10 1GE.
www.wru.co.uk

BEST DAY

WALES HAVE 10 Grand Slams but one in particular that stands out was in 1978, when a 16-7 victory over France delivered their third Grand Slam of a golden decade for a golden generation of Welshmen. The match was the final game for Gareth Edwards and Phil Bennett (right).

18TH MAR 1978

WORST DAY

WELSH RUGBY went into decline in the 1980s but the worst day for the country was saved for the start of the next decade when a once-proud rugby nation lost to Western Samoa, knocking them out of the 1991 World Cup (right). They lost 16-13, the superb Samoan defence to the fore.

6TH OCT 1991

FIRST TEST MATCH

WALES' TEST history got off to an awful start in 1881, the same year the Welsh Rugby Union was formed. Their first international was against England at Blackheath and they lost by a massive seven goals, one drop goal and six tries to nil! They waited until 1890 to beat England.

19TH FEB 1881

STAT ATTACK

Second-row Gareth Llewellyn enjoyed the longest Test career in Wales' history, winning 92 caps as he played for 15 years from 1989 to 2004.

FIVE GREAT PLAYERS

1. GARETH EDWARDS: The general who took Wales through their most successful period in the 1970s. A devastating passer, quick over the ground, Edwards was a genius who would have prospered in any era.

2. GARETH THOMAS: The first Welshman to win 100 caps, Thomas enjoyed a 12-year Test career that took in three World Cups, and ended with him becoming Wales' leading try-scorer.

3. CLIFF MORGAN: A genius in the No 10 shirt, Morgan was the forerunner to so many of the great Welsh outside-halves. Always played with flair.

4. BARRY JOHN: The Cardiff outside-half mesmerised defences in the early 1970s as Wales developed a team that was revered all over the world.

5. SHANE WILLIAMS: The speedster from Neath overtook Gareth Thomas's record in 2008 to become Wales' leading try-scorer of all time. The heart of a lion and twinkle toes.

GROUNDS

WALES PLAY their home matches at the 74,500-capacity Millennium Stadium in Cardiff, which is on the site of the old National Stadium in the centre of Cardiff.

South Africa were the side chosen to open the Millennium Stadium, which at the time was the largest in the UK, in 1999, providing Wales with an opening-day victory, 29-19, centre Mark Taylor privileged to be the first try-scorer at the ground.

In the early days following their first Test match in 1881, Wales toured the country playing home matches in Swansea, Llanelli and Newport. As recently as 2003, as Wales prepared for the World Cup, they made the trip north to play Romania at the Racecourse Ground.

COUNTRIES

AUSTRALIA

THE FIRST country to do a World Cup double, lifting the Webb Ellis Cup in 1991 and 1999, the Australians were one of the quickest countries to adapt to the game's new professional era, which began to take hold at the start of the 1990s.

A sport-mad country, Australia has always punched above its weight at the Olympic Games, the Australians prospering in rugby union despite a tiny playing base. There are fewer than 30,000 adults playing rugby in Australia compared to a whopping 150,000 in England!

After playing their first Test match in 1899, Australia struggled to establish themselves as a major rugby nation, faring badly in a number of Test series with their nearest rivals, South Africa and New Zealand.

Australia first played New Zealand in 1903, only recording a series victory for the first time in 1929, and between 1936 and 1980 it was almost New Zealand all the way with just one series going to Australia.

But all that changed in the 1980s and 1990s when a new breed of Australian rugby player burst onto the scene, the side completing a Grand Slam of victories over England, Wales, Scotland and Ireland on one tour in 1984.

The nucleus of this team, which contained Wallaby legends like Michael Lynagh, Nick Farr-Jones and David Campese, went on to win the World Cup in 1991, giving the new generation of Australian rugby players role models on which to build their careers. In 2007 Australia appointed their first Kiwi (Robbie Deans) as coach as they started on the road to the 2011 World Cup.

DID YOU KNOW?
Australia's record score in a Test match was the 142-0 hammering they handed out to Namibia at the 2003 Rugby World Cup.

Quick stats

TEAM COLOURS: Green and Gold
NICKNAME: Wallabies
HONOURS: World Cup winners (1991, 1999); Tri-Nations champions (2000, 2001)
ADDRESS: Australian Rugby Union, Ground Floor, 29-57 Christie Street, St Leonards NSW 2065

www.rugby.com.au

George Gregan was the first Australian to win 100 caps...David Campese the first to score 50 tries... and Michael Lynagh the first to kick 900 Test points.

BEST DAY

THE FIRST great Australian team was born in the mid-1980s when players like David Campese, Nick Farr-Jones (right) and Michael Lynagh burst onto the scene. Moulded by coach Bob Dwyer (far right) this side came of age in 1991 beating England 10-3 in the second World Cup Final.

2ND NOV 1991

WORST DAY

THE LOWEST day in Australian rugby history came in 1973 when the Wallabies lost to Tonga 11-16. The Tongans scored twice on the blind side of the scrum and four tries in all, although Australia actually led 11-8 with 10 minutes left. It remains their only defeat to Tonga.

30TH JUNE 1973

FIRST TEST MATCH

AUSTRALIA PLAYED their first Test match in the final year of the 19th century, against the touring side from Great Britain. In a four-Test series played in Sydney and Brisbane, Australia won the first Test 13-3 at the Sydney Cricket Ground, and wore light blue shirts for the game.

24TH JUNE 1899

STAT ATTACK

In 1998 when Jonny Wilkinson made his first start for England, Australia recorded an incredible 76-0 win, Stephen Larkham led with a hat-trick.

GROUNDS

THE WALLABIES play at a variety of stadiums around the country, the length and breadth from Perth in the west to Sydney in the east, as they try to spread the word about rugby, and overtake rugby league or Aussie Rules as the dominant sport.

Some of these include Subiaco Oval in Perth, Suncorp Stadium in Brisbane, Telstra Stadium in Sydney, and the MCG and the Telstra Dome in Melbourne.

In 2000 an incredible 109,874 people packed into the Telstra Stadium, where the World Cup Final was held three years later, to watch New Zealand grab a thrilling 39-35 victory, courtesy of a late Jonah Lomu try. This game is sometimess referred to as the greatest game of rugby ever played.

FIVE GREAT PLAYERS

1. GEORGE GREGAN: When the Zambian-born scrum-half retired in 2007, he had won an incredible 139 caps, a world record for any player.

2. MICHAEL LYNAGH: Known as Noddy to his friends, Lynagh was an exceptional outside-half who sparked the side into their World Cup triumph in 1991. Scored 911 points in an illustrious career.

3. DAVID CAMPESE: A genius who left an indelible mark on the game. Scorer of an incredible 64 tries in his 101 Tests, he was a maverick who lit up the rugby world for more than a decade.

4. JOHN EALES: Nicknamed Nobody because Nobody's perfect, Eales was captain of Australia when they won the World Cup in 1999. A genius in the lineout, he also kicked goals.

5. STEPHEN LARKHAM: The third Wallaby to win 100 caps, Larkham was at the centre of the World Cup triumph in 1999. Supreme No 10.

RECORDBREAKER

SEAN FITZPATRICK

In his career Sean Fitzpatrick won every honour on offer: World Cup, Tri-Nations, Super 12 and a Lions series win.

IN RUGBY union there are tough players you would always rather have with you than against you. New Zealand's most capped hooker Sean Fitzpatrick falls into that category.

Teak-tough in his play, he never took a backward step in his 11-year Test career that brought him 92 caps, 51 as captain of New Zealand.

Once Fitzy had got his hands on the All Blacks No 2 jersey, after an injury to Andy Dalton before the start of the 1987 World Cup, it was almost impossible to wrest it from his grasp. He still holds the world record for number of consecutive Test matches played: 63, that run only ending when he was rested for a match against Japan.

In his career he won every honour there was on offer. A World Cup winners' medal in 1987 was followed, when the game went professional, by a Tri-Nations Championship in 1996, the same year he helped the Auckland Blues to the inaugural Super 12 title.

In terms of the one-off series, Fitzpatrick (who took the All Blacks captaincy in 1992) also reigned supreme, being a crucial part of the All Blacks side that inflicted a series defeat on the 1993 British & Irish Lions. He also became the first New Zealander to captain his country to a series win in South Africa, the All Blacks' oldest and fiercest rivals.

An icon of New Zealand rugby, the All Blacks won 74 out of the 92 games he played. Fitzpatrick was awarded the New Zealand Order of Merit by the Governor General in 1997, a year before his career was ended by a knee injury.

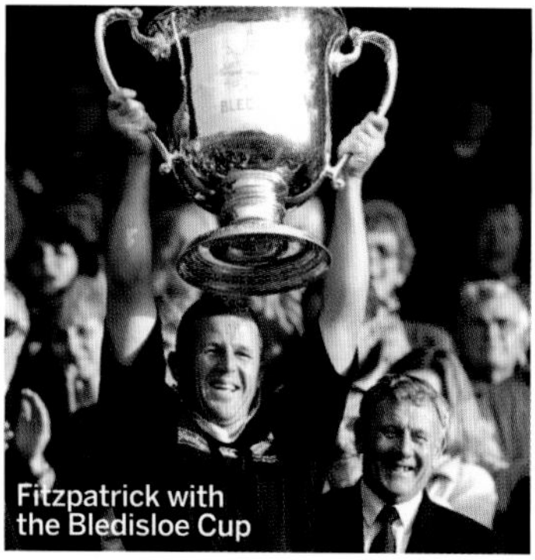
Fitzpatrick with the Bledisloe Cup

Fact file

Full name: Sean Brian Thomas Fitzpatrick
Date of birth: 4 June, 1963
Place of birth: Auckland, New Zealand
Nickname: Fitzy
School: Sacred Heart College
Position: Hooker
First cap: 1986 v France
Test caps: 92
Test points: 60

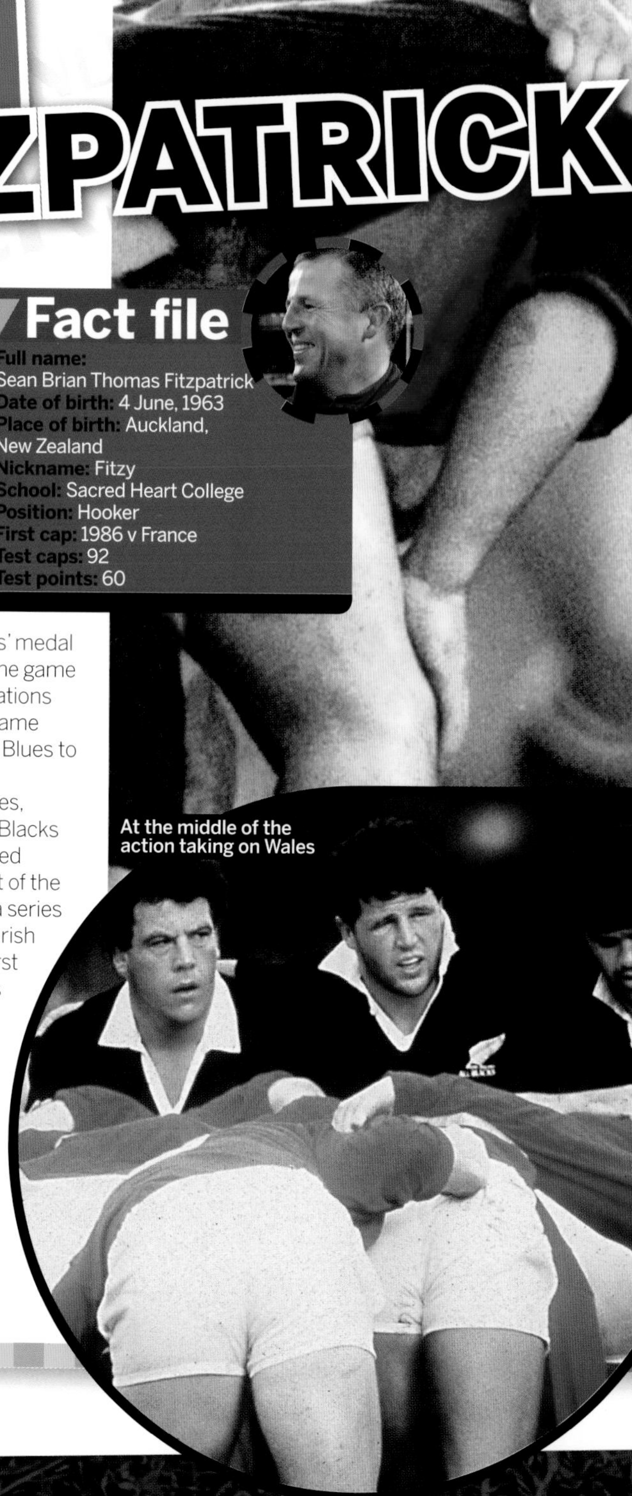
At the middle of the action taking on Wales

DID YOU KNOW?

Sean Fitzpatrick comes from a rugby-playing family, his father Brian (BBJ) playing three times for New Zealand in 1950s, in a career that was blighted by injury.

5 UNFORGETTABLE DAYS

28TH JUN 1986

1 THE ALL Blacks are in disarray before Fitzy's debut v France, as so many players had been banned playing for the Cavaliers but the Baby Blacks still win.

20TH JUN 1987

2 DAVID KIRK lifts the trophy as captain but Sean Fitzpatrick has a huge part to play as New Zealand win the first World Cup tournament.

3RD JUL 1993

3 ONE OF Fitzpatrick's proudest moments as a captain, leading the All Blacks to a win over the British & Irish Lions, 30-13 in the final game in Auckland.

18TH JUN 1995

4 AN INCREDIBLE day to be New Zealand captain as Jonah Lomu scores four tries against England as the All Blacks win the semi-final.

24TH AUG 1996

5 NO NEW Zealand team had ever won a series in South Africa until Fitzpatrick's Class of 1996 rolled into town, winning 2-1, the second in Pretoria to clinch it, 33-26.

RECORDBREAKER

ENGLAND RUGBY®

STAT ATTACK

Jonny Wilkinson broke the record for most dropped goals in Test matches, in 2008, when he scored his 29th, overtaking the previous mark of Naas Botha.

5 UNFORGETTABLE DAYS

1 JONNY WILKINSON made his England debut as a teenager in 1998, coming on at wing in the 35-17 victory over Ireland, when he was just 18 years of age. His first start came in June.

4TH APR 1998

2 JONNY'S FIRST big impact on the world stage came in June 2000 when he kicked all of England's points in their 27-22 win against South Africa in Bloemfontein.

24TH JUN 2000

3 HIS GREATEST day undoubtedly came in 2003 when he kicked England to World Cup glory in the final against Australia in Sydney, dropping a goal with only a few seconds left.

22ND NOV 2003

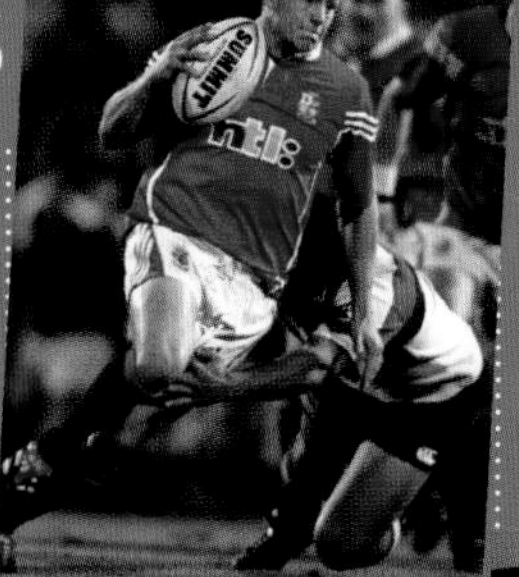

4 JONNY ALWAYS had an ambition to be a British & Irish Lion and that dream came true in 2001 when he was picked for the tour to Australia, playing in all three Tests.

30TH JUN 2001

5 A PROLIFIC points scorer, Jonny became the first Englishman to score 1,000 points in Test matches for one country in his side's 23-19 victory over Italy in 2008.

10TH FEB 2008

JONNY WILKINSON

Fact file

Full name: Jonathan Peter Wilkinson
Date of birth: 25 May, 1979
Place of birth: Frimley, Surrey, England, United Kingdom
Height: 5ft 9in (1.77m)
Weight: 13st 12lbs (88kg)
Nickname: Wilko
School: Lord Wandsworth College
Position: Fly-half, inside-centre
First cap: 1998 v Ireland

JONNY WILKINSON became the most famous rugby player on the planet in 2003, when he kicked a drop goal (with 20 seconds left) to win the World Cup for England, the first such triumph by a side from Europe.

The wonder boy from Newcastle has ice-cool nerves, and he demonstrated it best of all in the final as he slotted the kick not with his favoured left foot but with his right!

After winning the World Cup in 2003, Wilkinson's career was dogged by a series of injuries that would have finished many players. He missed every England game in 2004, 2005 and 2006 through those injuries, which affected almost every part of his body, including shoulder, bicep, knee, groin, ankle and kidneys.

But he put all of them behind him in January 2007, coming back into the England team, under new coach Brian Ashton, to score a 'full house' of try, conversion, penalty and drop goal in a stunning 42-20 win over Scotland at Twickenham.

yer for both
ft) and
(below)

'I can't say enough about Wilko. He is a very special player, a very special person,' said England captain in 2003, Martin Johnson.

Wilkinson played in his third World Cup in 2007, taking a crucial role as England made the final for the second tournament running, only this time their journey ended in heartache as they lost 15-6 to South Africa.

A Newcastle Falcon for the whole of his professional career, Wilkinson was spotted as a teenager by Newcastle coaches Rob Andrew and Steve Bates, who convinced him to make the move north, out of the spotlight.

Admired by team-mates and opponents alike, once England had won the World Cup in 2003 skipper Martin Johnson said of him: 'I can't say enough about Wilko, he was sensational. He is a very special player, a very special person.'

In 2003 after the World Cup he became the IRB World Player of the Year and the youngest ever rugby union player to receive an MBE, picking up an OBE a year later. In 2008 he finally became the world record points-scorer, overtaking Neil Jenkins' 1,090, against Scotland.

His 29th drop goal, in 2008, a new world record

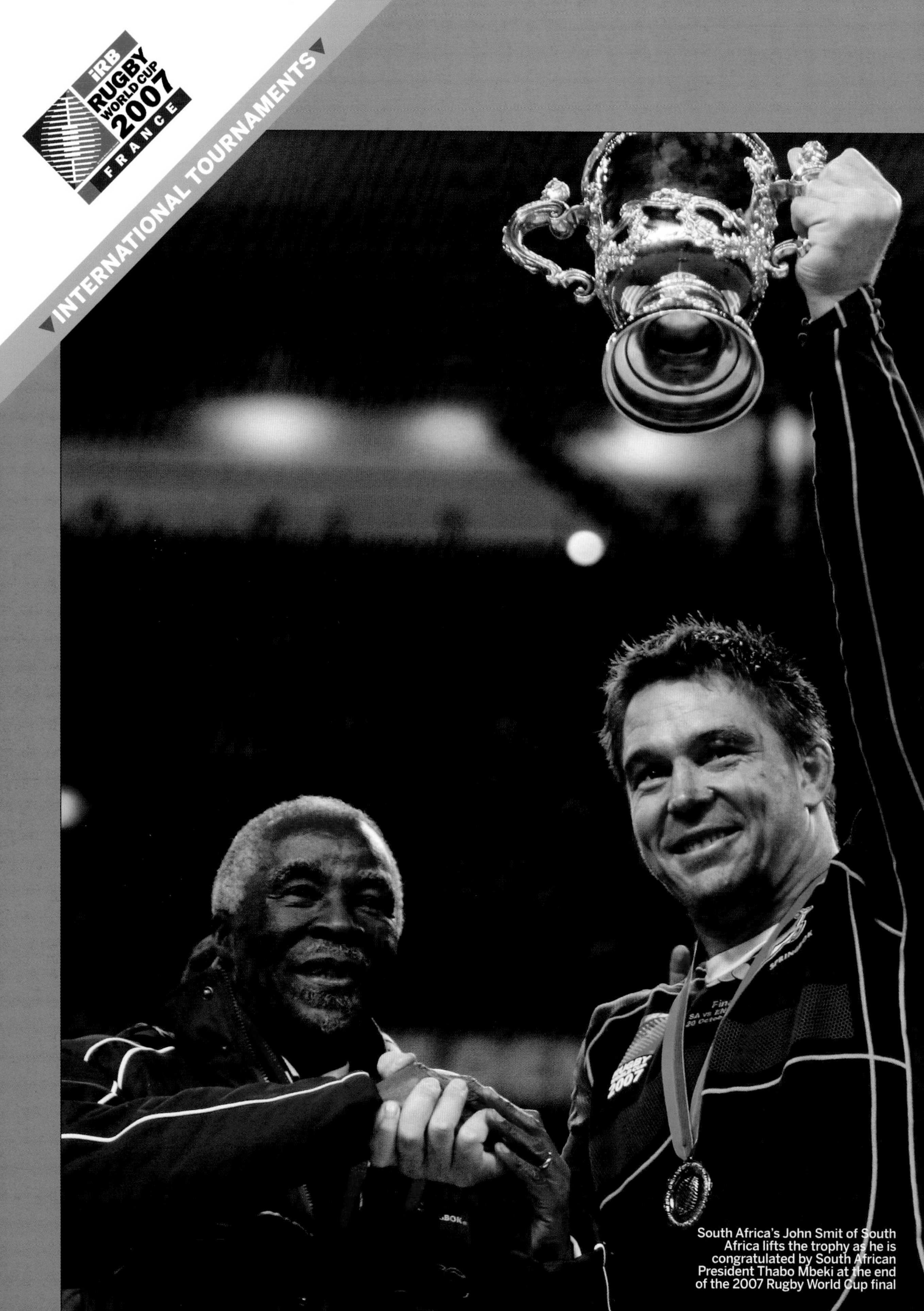

South Africa's John Smit of South Africa lifts the trophy as he is congratulated by South African President Thabo Mbeki at the end of the 2007 Rugby World Cup final

DID YOU KNOW? England's Jason Leonard holds the record (22) for most appearances in the finals.

THE RUGBY WORLD CUP

It is the most prized possession in the rugby world. Once every four years the best sides on the planet fight for the Webb Ellis Cup.

WHEN SOUTH Africa lifted the Webb Ellis Cup in 2007, they did it in front of a global television audience of three billion, winning a tournament watched by more than two million spectators, such has been the effect of the Rugby World Cup.

The game resisted a worldwide tournament for decades before the International Rugby Board finally acceded to the demands of Australia and New Zealand to host a tournament every four years, as soccer has done since 1930.

The first Rugby World Cup came in 1987 and, despite its worldwide television audience of 300 million, it had a limited impact on the rest of the sporting world. But in the 20 years that followed, the tournament has grown beyond anyone's expectations and it is now the third biggest global sporting event behind the Olympics and the FIFA World Cup.

New Zealand may only have won the tournament once, in 1987, but they have more victories in the Finals stages than any other team, with 30 in the six World Cups. Australia come next with 28 wins, then France on 26. Unfortunately for the All Blacks, many of those victories have been in the group stages of the tournament, ▶

WORLD CUP FINALS

1987 - New Zealand 29 France 9
Final: Eden Park, New Zealand

1991 - Australia 9 England 6
Final: Twickenham, England

1995 - South Africa 15 New Zealand 12
Final: Ellis Park, South Africa (right)

1999 - Australia 35 France 12
Final: Millennium Stadium, Wales

2003 - England 20 Australia 17
Final: Telstra Stadium, Australia

2007 - South Africa 15 England 6
Final: Stade de France, France

It's there...Jonny Wilkinson celebrates the late drop goal that won the 2003 World Cup

▶ and when it has come to the knockout stages the New Zealanders have come up short.

Two sides, Australia and South Africa, have won the World Cup twice, as the tournament became dominated by the sides from the southern hemisphere. In, fact it took until the fifth World Cup (2003) for a side from the northern hemisphere (England) to win it.

That domination is hardly surprising considering a World Cup was the idea of both the Australia and New Zealand rugby unions, and when it was suggested for the first time in the early 1980s there was serious opposition from Europe. The southern hemisphere sides were also far quicker to embrace the new challenges of professionalism.

The tournament, which lasts around six weeks, ran through a number of formats before settling on a 20-team competition, putting the sides into four groups of five, the top two in each group progressing to the quarter-finals.

South Africa's victory in 2007 gave them the best winning percentage, in the tournament, of any side in world rugby. Banned from the tournaments in 1987 and 1991 because of their apartheid political regime, they have subsequently won two of the four World Cups they have entered. ▶

DID YOU KNOW?

South Africa's **Victor Matfield** was the man of the match in the 2007 World Cup final, following England's **Jonny Wilkinson** who took the honour in 2003 after his winning drop goal.

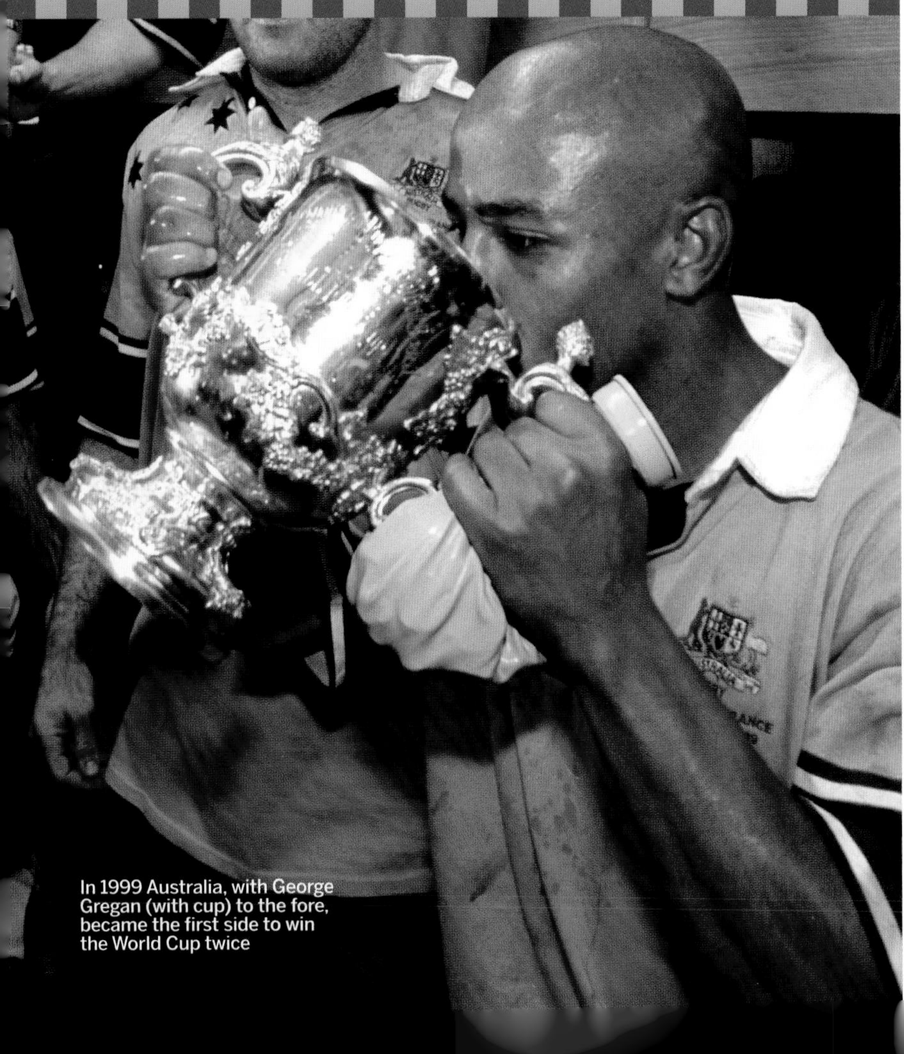

In 1999 Australia, with George Gregan (with cup) to the fore, became the first side to win the World Cup twice

THE POINTS MACHINES

NEW ZEALAND's legendary Superboot, Grant Fox, still holds the record for most points scored in one World Cup tournament, setting an incredible record of 126 points at the first World Cup in 1987. Below are the men who ended the first six World Cups as the leading points-scorer.

1987
1 GRANT FOX
New Zealand (126 points)

1991
2 RALPH KEYES
Ireland (78)

1995
3 THIERRY LACROIX
France (112)

1999
4 GONZALO QUESADA
Argentina (102)

2003
5 JONNY WILKINSON
England (113)

2007
6 PERCY MONTGOMERY
South Africa (105)

In 1995 South Africa beat New Zealand on home soil and in 2007 they travelled to Europe to lift the trophy in Paris' Stade de France.

The future for the World Cup will bring a return to New Zealand in 2011 after they beat off a challenge from one of the emerging nations, Japan, to stage the seventh event.

The men of the rugby world aren't the only ones to stage a World Cup and women have been playing in their IRB-sanctioned tournament since 1998. Unlike in the men's game, there was only one winner in the first three tournaments: New Zealand, or the Black Ferns (below, right) as they are known. Before the IRB backed the Women's World Cup, the USA were the first champions in 1991, England following them to the title in Edinburgh, in 1994.

DID YOU KNOW?
One woman led New Zealand to a hat-trick of world titles from 1998...Farah Palmer.

POINTS MAKE **PRIZES**

JONNY WILKINSON has played in three World Cups, in 1999, 2003 and 2007, and no player has scored more points than the Englishman, as he overtook Gavin Hastings. Wilkinson and Hastings, who also played in three tournaments in 1987, 1991 and 1995, are the only players to go through the 200-point mark. The top four are:

JONNY WILKINSON
ENGLAND: 249 points, 1999-2007

GAVIN HASTINGS
SCOTLAND: 227 points, 1987-1995

MICHAEL LYNAGH
AUSTRALIA: 195 points, 1987-1995

GRANT FOX
NEW ZEALAND: 170 points, 1987-1991

Bryan Habana (left) and Jonah Lomu (above) set the try-scoring standard in the World Cup

TRY-LINE TERRORS

THE GREAT Jonah Lomu saved some of his best rugby for World Cup finals and, even though he never managed to win the tournament, he scored a sensational 15 tries in the two competitions in which he starred.

Lomu scored four tries to knock out England in the 1995 semi-final, crossing the try-line eight times overall in that tournament, a record that was matched in 2007 by Springboks star Bryan Habana.

The leading scorers in one tournament are:

1. BRYAN HABANA
South Africa
8 tries in 2007

2. JONAH LOMU
New Zealand
8 tries in 1999

3. MARC ELLIS
New Zealand
7 tries in 1995

4. MILS MULIAINA
New Zealand
7 tries in 2003

5. DREW MITCHELL
Australia
7 tries in 2007

6. DOUG HOWLETT
New Zealand
7 tries in 2007

IRB
RUGBY WORLD CUP 2011
INTERNATIONAL TOURNAMENTS
EDEN PARK
EDEN PARK
RE/MAX
Cayman Isla

THE RUGBY WORLD CUP 2011

DID YOU KNOW?
In the bidding for the 2011 World Cup, Japan came second in the voting and South Africa third.

The seventh Rugby World Cup will be held in New Zealand, 24 years after the Webb Ellis Cup was contested for the first time.

THERE IS a certain symmetry about the World Cup in 2011 as the tournament will return to its roots. Back in 1987, when the Rugby World Cup was in its infancy, it was held in New Zealand (and Australia), so for the next tournament in 2011 it is time to go back to the land of the All Blacks.

England, South Africa, Wales, Australia and France have hosted the tournament since the first one, so it is now time to let New Zealand have another crack at rugby's greatest show on earth.

One thing is for sure: the 2011 event will have very little in common with the 1987 competition, as almost everything has changed in the game of rugby in those 24 years.

Most significantly, rugby has turned professional in the years since 1987, which has meant a totally different approach both on and off the field.

In 2011, despite attempts to reduce it to 16, the Rugby World Cup 2011 tournament will comprise 20 teams. The playing window for RWC 2011 in New Zealand is September to October 2011 with the final taking place on the weekend of October 22-23 at Eden Park (above, left).

The New Zealand Government has also announced that the school holidays in 2011 will be delayed by two weeks for all students in the country, to coincide with the final two weeks of the World Cup.

The 2011 qualification structure is presently being reviewed but it has already been announced that the number of automatic qualifiers has increased from eight to 12 places. Therefore, South Africa, England, Argentina, France, Australia, New Zealand, Scotland, Fiji, Wales, Ireland, Tonga and Italy have automatically qualified for 2011 World Cup after finishing in the top three in their respective World Cup 2007 pools.

The qualification system for the remaining eight places began in the Caribbean in April 2008.

The host nation Cayman Islands played Trinidad & Tobago on April 20 in the first match of the championship (see opposite page, below), and eventually it was Trinidad & Tobago who won the Caribbean tournament to progress to the next round of qualification. This was six months to the day after a global audience of billions watched the World Cup 2007 final in France, when South Africa became world champions, by beating England.

THE SIX NATIONS

THE GREATEST annual rugby tournament in the world, the RBS 6 Nations is revered in every corner of the planet where the great game of rugby is played.

Starting out in 1883 as a four nations tournament featuring England, Scotland, Wales and Ireland, France made it a Five Nations tournament in 1910, Italy becoming the most recent country to join the family in 2000.

It is by far the most prized annual rugby tournament, playing to sell-out crowds and tens of millions on TV, it is the envy of the world.

England and Wales have enjoyed the lion's share of the success, closely followed by France as the title of the dominant nation in the Championship has ebbed and flowed through the decades.

NO BONUS
The Six Nations is almost on its own in rejecting bonus points. It is a simple two points for a win, one for a draw.

AMAZING RECORDS

The championship has seen some incredible performances over the years, since the first one kicked off in 1883. Here are some of the best.

1. TRY SCORERS

In 1914 England's Cyril Lowe set a record for scoring eight tries in one Championship, a mark that was equalled in 1924 by Scotland's Ian Smith, but no one has got near since!

2. POINTS GALORE

ITALY'S ARRIVAL in 2000 gave sides a chance to set new records and England wasted no time posting a record number of points in one championship in 2001 (229) and the record number of points in one match, against Italy, when they won 80-23.

3. HE'S A RECORD BREAKER

JONNY WILKINSON holds more championship records than any other player in the history of the game. Some of them are:

- Most points in a season: 89 in 2001
- Most points in a match: 35 in 2001 v Italy
- Most penalties in a season: 18 in 2000

TWO SLAMS IN A ROW

Back-to-back Grand Slams are rare and have been achieved five times: by Wales in 1908 & 1909, by England three times in 1913 & 1914, 1923 & 1924 and 1991 & 1992 and France in 1997 & 1998.

France celebrate their back-to-back Grand Slams in 1998

France in 2004 (left) and Wales in 2005 (right) celebrate their Grand Slam triumphs

▶ History dictates there are a number of competitions within the Six Nations, which include every Scotland v England game being contested for the Calcutta Cup, France and Italy playing for the Giuseppe Garibaldi Trophy, and England and Ireland battling it out for the Millennium Trophy.

The Championship's roots as a Home Nations tournament are also reflected in the competition for the Triple Crown each year, awarded if one home nation beats the other three. And of course there is the dreaded wooden spoon, not actually presented as a trophy but spiritually given to the country that finishes last in the table.

The wooden spoon is a modern-day invention because until 1994 sides that finished on equal points at the end of a campaign were not separated by points difference. And in fact the Five Nations committee didn't even award a trophy until 1993, France getting their hands on it first, followed by the Welsh.

Before the days of the winner being decided on points difference it was normal for two or three countries to share top spot.

▼GRAND SLAMMERS

WHEN WALES won a Grand Slam, beating every other country in the Six Nations Championship in 2008, they were the 34th side to do it, since they recorded the first one back in 1908.

It wasn't called the Grand Slam in those days as the term wasn't accepted until England's triumph of 1957 but, the celebrations were probably as fervent when England, Scotland, Ireland and France lost to Wales more than a century ago.

THE GRAND SLAM WINNERS HAVE BEEN:
England (12): 1913, 1914, 1921, 1923, 1924, 1928, 1957, 1980, 1991, 1992, 1995 and 2003 (above).
Wales (10): 1908, 1909, 1911, 1950, 1952, 1971, 1976, 1978, 2005 and 2008.
France (8): 1968, 1977, 1981, 1987, 1997, 1998, 2002 and 2004.
Scotland (3): 1925, 1984, 1990.
Ireland (1): 1948
Italy (0)

But the most prized possession for any international team is not the Championship but the Grand Slam, given to a side that has a perfect record of five wins in a particular season, confirming absolute domination for that country.

The term Grand Slam wasn't even invented until Sale's Eric Evans led England to a clean sweep in 1957 and the phrase was coined by newspapers of the day.

The Evans Grand Slam was England's seventh but came nine years after Ireland's one and only Slam in 1948, inspired by Karl Mullen, Jackie Kyle and a host of Irishmen who have gone down in folklore.

If few will forget Kyle and his men of the late 1940s the same can be said of perhaps the most famous team to play in the Championship: the Welsh side of the 1970s. With legendary players like Gareth Edwards, Barry John, JPR Williams and Mervyn Davies, they won three Grand Slams, six championships and the Triple Crown five times in quick succession, to dominate the game in that era.

England had two periods of great success, in the 1920s and when a young Will Carling was put in ▶

certain Will Carling was appointed captain of the side in the late 1980s, presiding over a period when England won three Grand Slams.

The Scots have collected three Grand Slams in their history. The last of these in 1990 was the sweetest as they went into the final game against England with both sides capable of winning the ultimate prize.

The Six Nations effectively has seven other divisions, the second being known as the European Nations Cup, although there is no promotion or relegation between the two divisions. It is staged on a biannual basis; the competition running in 2007 and 2008 was won by Georgia, in a division containing Czech Republic, Georgia, Portugal, Romania, Russia and Spain.

The Women's Six Nations synchronised its fixtures with the men in 2007, when Spain took over from Italy as the sixth team.

In recent years England's women's team has dominated the tournament, winning a hat-trick of Grand Slams from 2006 to 2008, the last one under the captaincy of Worcester's Catherine Spencer and coached by Gary Street.

England's women are delighted with their 2007 Grand Slam

TROPHY HUNTERS

IN THE first 100 years of the Championship points difference wasn't used to separate the sides. If two or more teams finished on the same number of points, the Championship was shared.

In 1973 the results incredibly left all five nations, England, Wales, Scotland, Ireland and France, with two wins so the Championship was declared a five-way tie.

The last sides to share the Championship were Wales and France in 1988.

A trophy was introduced in 1994, and Wales captain Ieuan Evans was given the privilege of being the first captain since the first Championship in 1883 to lift a trophy!

THE WINNERS OF THE LAST 20 CHAMPIONSHIPS WERE:

1989: France
1990: Scotland
1991: England
1992: England
1993: France
1994: Wales
1995: England
1996: England
1997: France
1998: France
1999: Scotland
2000: England
2001: England
2002: France
2003: England
2004: France
2005: Wales
2006: France
2007: France
2008: Wales

MATCH BAN
France were kicked out of the Championship in 1931 over allegations of professionalism, and only came back in 1947.

Andy Nicol celebrates as Scotland rob England of a Grand Slam with defeat on the final day of the 2000 Championship

France were champions, but without a Grand Slam in 2007

Wales though picked up a Slam in 2008, while...

...Romania took the European Nations Cup in 2006

THE TRI-NATIONS

WHEN RUGBY turned professional in 1995, it was inevitable that the giants of the southern hemisphere would look north and attempt to stage a competition that rivalled the Six Nations. Finances also demanded a more regular tournament than New Zealand, South Africa and Australia had played before, a massive television deal bank-rolling so much of the game down south.

Three of the most powerful rugby nations in the world meet in an annual tournament that captivates the rugby world in July and August.

And so the Tri-Nations was born in the boardrooms of the All Blacks, Wallabies and Springboks, with a £360million television deal to ensure the success of rugby in the new Tri-Nations format.

South Africa and New Zealand, in particular, had enjoyed some titantic Test series, going back to 1921, but all this rivalry was condensed into a series of games, usually held in July and August, following on from the Super 12 and the arrival, in June, of the northern hemisphere sides for their annual tours.

Considering their record in the ensuing seasons, the first game (in 1996) was fittingly a victory for New ▶

AMAZING RECORDS

The Tri-Nations has seen some incredible performances since the first one kicked off in 1996. Here are some of the most amazing.

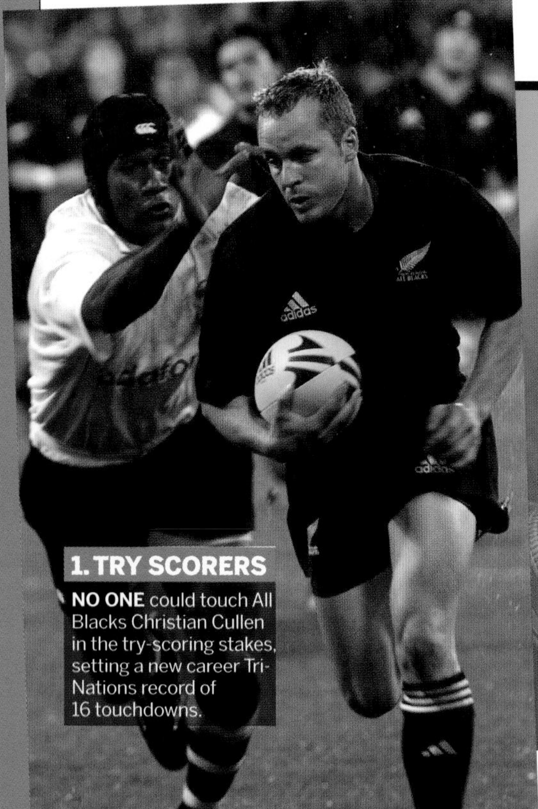

1. TRY SCORERS

NO ONE could touch All Blacks Christian Cullen in the try-scoring stakes, setting a new career Tri-Nations record of 16 touchdowns.

2. POINTS GALORE

IN KICKING terms Andrew Mehrtens (above) was untouchable in the early years of the Tri-Nations. The Canterbury Crusader was the first player in the Tri-Nations to:

- Score 300 career points
- Score more than 80 penalties & 15 cons
- Score 29 points in one match

3. MAKE MINE A TRIPLE

HAT-TRICKS are hard to come by in the Tri-Nations, with none until the 2003 season. The first three players to score them were:

- Joe Rokocoko, NZ v Aus, Sydney 2003
- Marius Joubert, SA v NZ, Jo'burg 2004
- Doug Howlett, NZ v Aus, Auckland 2005

DID YOU KNOW?
Joel Stransky was the first to score 25 points in a Tri-Nations game against Australia in 1996.

Doug Howlett (left) with the Bledisloe Cup and Joe Rokocoko with the Tri-Nations trophy, in 2007

TRI NATIONS

South Africa's first Tri-Nations Grand Slam arrived in 1998

Australia had an exceptional team in 2000 and 2001, captained by John Eales (left)

DID YOU KNOW?

New Zealand set a new Tri-Nations points-scoring record in 2006 with a massive 179 in their winning campaign. They still didn't beat the record of most tries, which is held by South Africa's 18 in 1997.

Zealand as the All Blacks scored six tries against Australia to win 43-6.

The tournament has been a rousing success and, although it doesn't have the history of the Six Nations to fall back on, it does have some fantastic rugby.

New Zealand have dominated the Tri-Nations, winning eight of the first 12 titles, completing a Grand Slam (a season in which they won every game) in 1996, 1997 and 2003, stressing their domination of the rugby world...except, of course, when it comes to World Cups.

In fact, the winner of the Tri-Nations has never gone on to win the World Cup, New Zealand winning the tournament in 1999, 2003 and 2007 but failing to get beyond the semi-finals of that year's World Cup.

The All Blacks haven't had it all their own way though, and South Africa completed a Grand Slam of their own in 1998. In a tournament where sides have to contend with massive time differences, an away win is a precious commodity.

Much to the relief of many rugby commentators, South Africa bucked the New Zealand trend in 1998, as it looked to many that the result of the tournament might be a foregone conclusion.

In 1998 South Africa's Tri-Nations victory came in the middle of their 17-match, world record-equalling run.

Normal service was resumed in 1999 as New Zealand took the title back but an exceptional Australian team, perhaps the best in their history, then won back-to-back titles, in 2000 and 2001, to prove the Tri-Nations tournament was truly a three-nation competition.

South Africa were in great form in 1997

THE 50-POINTERS

IN 1997, South Africa were the first side to score 60 points in a Tri-Nations match when they hammered Australia, 61-22, in Pretoria. This is the highest score against Australia in a Test match ever.

The first four teams to score 50 points or more in a Tri-Nations game were:

1. South Africa in 1997, beating Australia in Pretoria, 61-22
2. New Zealand in 1997, beating South Africa in Auckland, 55-35
3. New Zealand in 2003, beating South Africa in Pretoria, 52-16
4. New Zealand in 2003, beating Australia in Sydney, 50-21

- In 2006 Australia couldn't have come any closer to beating the 50-points mark as they thrashed South Africa in Brisbane 49-0!

▶ The 2000 competition, in particular, was a cracker with Australia only sealing the title with away wins in South Africa (19-18) and New Zealand (24-23), captain John Eales grabbing the victory against the All Blacks with a last-minute penalty.

The crowds have also flocked to games, with a staggering 109,874 people crammed into the Olympic Stadium in 2000 to watch one of the greatest games the rugby world has even seen, with All Black Jonah Lomu swooping to score a winning try in the final minutes as New Zealand won the game 39-35.

In 2006 the Tri-Nations changed format. Up until then the tournament was run with teams playing on a home and away basis, but in 2006 an extra round was added, the teams playing each other three times.

Another way of invigorating the format would be to follow the Six Nations Championship and invite a new team into the tournament. A Pacific Islands team was rejected, while Argentina's campaign to gain entry into the tournament has fallen on deaf ears. As in the Six Nations, a number of other competitions are run within the Tri-Nations.

Every time Australia and New Zealand play each other the Bledisloe Cup is on offer, while South Africa and Australia play for the Mandela Trophy.

DID YOU KNOW?
It's four points for a win in the Tri-Nations and a bonus for scoring four tries in one match.

South Africa (above) celebrate in 2004...and it's Australia's turn in 2001 (below left), while New Zealand take centre stage with a victory in 2007 (below right)

New Zealand celebrate another Tri-Nations win, this time in 1996, dominating the tournament for the first decade

THE WINNERS

SINCE NEW Zealand won the first Tri-Nations tournament in 1996, they have dominated the competition that decides which is the best side in the southern hemisphere. In the first 12 years New Zealand completed a Grand Slam three times, in 1996, 1997 and 2003. Australia have never completed a Grand Slam and South Africa did it once, in 1998.

THE FULL LIST OF WINNERS IS:

1996: New Zealand
1997: New Zealand
1998: South Africa
1999: New Zealand
2000: Australia
2001: Australia
2002: New Zealand
2003: New Zealand
2004: South Africa
2005: New Zealand
2006: New Zealand
2007: New Zealand

INTERNATIONAL TOURNAMENTS

THE LIONS

Perhaps the most famous team in the rugby world, the British and Irish Lions have a rich history dating back to the 19th century.

The Lions team is made up of the best players from England, Wales, Scotland and Ireland

The Waterford Crystal trophy won by New Zealand in 2005, for winning the Lions series

JOHN HOPKINS, the famous rugby writer from *The Times* newspaper, once described a Lions tour as a cross between a prep school outing and the Crusades, and in that analogy he summed up the essence of a trip by the most famous rugby team on the planet.

The Lions, who rarely play games in the United Kingdom or Ireland, have been touring the world since 1910, representing the rugby nations of England, Scotland, Ireland and Wales. Many refer to the side as the British Lions, a monicker that was finally ditched in 2001, as the side represents southern Ireland as well.

British and Irish teams had toured the southern hemisphere from 1888 but it wasn't until the 1910 trip that an official side was selected by a committee, representing the four home unions, to tour South Africa.

In that century Australia, South Africa and New Zealand have been regular hosts of the Lions, who have capped the best and most famous players from England, Wales, Scotland and Ireland. They have also made trips to Argentina and Sri Lanka and in 2005 even hosted Argentina at the Millennium Stadium, in Cardiff, to help raise funds for the trip to New Zealand that year. ▶

IF THE CAP FITS

THE BEST players from England, Wales, Scotland and Ireland have played for the Lions, so the records they hold are some of the most sought-after in the rugby world. Some players only get to play for the Lions once, as they tour every four years, so a career with four Tests is an achievement. Those who played most are:

WILLIE JOHN McBRIDE (left)
Ireland, 17 Tests from 1962-1974

DICKIE JEEPS
England, 13 Tests from 1955-1962

MIKE GIBSON
Wales, 12 Tests from 1966-1971

GRAHAM PRICE
Wales, 12 Tests from 1977-1983

TONY O'REILLY
Ireland, 10 Tests from 1955-1959

RHYS WILLIAMS
Wales, 10 Tests from 1955-1959

GARETH EDWARDS (right)
Wales, 10 Tests from 1968-1974

Lions fans have shown incredible devotion, tens of thousands travelling on each of the tours since 1997

THE LAST THREE TOURS

The 2005 Lions were hammered

1997 - SOUTH AFRICA

COACH: Ian McGeechan
CAPTAIN: Martin Johnson
The first professional Lions tour, after the game went 'open' two years before, was the last winning trip for the famous men in red. Led by Leicester captain Martin Johnson, the Lions won the Test series 2-1 after taking an unassailable lead in Durban.
FIRST TEST (Cape Town)
South Africa 16 Lions 25
SECOND TEST (Durban)
South Africa 15 Lions 18
THIRD TEST (Johannesburg)
South Africa 35 Lions 16

2001 - AUSTRALIA

COACH: Graham Henry
CAPTAIN: Martin Johnson
Before this tour began, Australia captain John Eales predicted the Lions series would be won by a side winning two consecutive Tests. And so it proved with the Lions going 1-0 up with a spectacular victory in Brisbane, before the Aussies pulled them back to take it.
FIRST TEST (Brisbane)
Australia 13 Lions 29
SECOND TEST (Melbourne)
Australia 35 Lions 14
THIRD TEST (Sydney)

2005 - NEW ZEALAND

COACH: Sir Clive Woodward
CAPTAIN: Brian O'Driscoll
The worst tour in Lions history, Sir Clive Woodward's team were hammered the length and breadth of New Zealand, losing all three Tests. The loss of Lawrence Dallaglio, captain Brian O'Driscoll and the influential Richard Hill to injury scuppered any chance of them being competitive.
FIRST TEST (Christchurch)
New Zealand 21 Lions 3
SECOND TEST (Wellington)
New Zealand 48 Lions 18
THIRD TEST (Auckland)
New Zealand 38 Lions 19

The 2001 Lions won the first Test only to lose the next two

▶ The Lions, coached by Sir Clive Woodward, suffered a record defeat on that 2005 trip to New Zealand, outclassed in every Test match, conceding a stunning 107 points in the three Tests to a side acknowledged as the best in the world at that time.

Tradition dictates that the Lions play their hosts in a three- or four-Test series but also play in a number of tour matches along the way. This schedule led to some Lions tours lasting six months, although modern-day trips are around six to eight weeks.

No one would recognise the Lions today unless they ran out in red but it hasn't always been that way. Early Lions teams played in dark blue, changing to their famous red shirts in 1930. They also started out life as the British Isles touring team, only adopting the Lions name between the wars, when the term was coined by newspapers.

After a succession of defeats, the team itself moved into a new era in 1955 when a side containing legends like Cliff Morgan, Dickie Jeeps, Jackie Kyle and Tony O'Reilly went to South Africa and earned a 2-2 draw in one of the hardest countries in the world to win Test matches at that time. On the whole tour the 1955 Lions emerged with one draw and 19 victories from the 25 fixtures.

The 1960s was an era best forgotten by the Lions, but in the 1970s two of the most famous sides to represent the British Isles journeyed to New Zealand in 1971 and to South Africa in 1974. The only dispute is which of these Lions sides was the best!

The 1971 Lions (captained by John Dawes) and the 1974 vintage (led by Willie John McBride) contained some of the same players, including Gareth Edwards and JPR Williams, but more importantly they had a spirit, passion and flair for the game that many believe has never been matched since by any other team. They played with panache and created a bond amongst the players that has stood the test of time. ▶

DID YOU KNOW?
The founding father of the British and Irish Lions is the **Arthur Shrewsbury** who took a touring side with **Alfred Shaw**, made up mostly of Englishmen, to Australia and New Zealand in 1888.

In 1989 the Lions beat Australia 2-1 in the Tests... but (below) lost 2-1 in New Zealand four years later

THE NEXT TRIP

IN 2009 the Lions will return to South Africa for what promises to be a titanic battle against the world champions. The tour dates are:

30 May: Highveld XV, Rustenburg; 3 June: Golden Lions, Johannesburg; 6 June: Free State Cheetahs, Bloemfontein; 10 June: Sharks, Durban; 13 June: Western Province, Cape Town; 16 or 17 June: Coastal XV, Port Elizabeth; 20 June: First Test, Durban; 23 June: Emerging Springboks, Cape Town; 27 June: Second Test, Pretoria; 4 July: Third Test, Johannesburg.

The 1971 side, which was coached by the visionary from Llanelli, Carwyn James, were the first Lions to win a Test series in New Zealand (2-1, with one draw). The 1974 team triumphed 3-0 with a draw in the Test series, remaining unbeaten on the whole trip, playing an energy-sapping 22 matches in total.

Despite the legacy of the Lions from the 1970s, and a great victory in Australia in 1989, many people (England captain Will Carling for one) regarded the Lions as a dying breed in the age of professional rugby, but instead of becoming extinct they have taken on an almost mythical status since the game turned professional in 1995. They have become the antidote to professional rugby and have developed a huge following from fans, some 30,000 travelling to Australia in 2001 to cheer on the men in red.

DID YOU KNOW?
The last time the Lions toured both Australia and New Zealand in the same year was 1971.

It helped that the first professional tour, to South Africa in 1997, was a winning tour, the Lions picking up the first two Tests to clinch the series before the final match. The 2009 trip, back to South Africa, is regarded as one of the biggest sporting events to take place in the republic. 'Lions tours just get bigger and bigger,' explained Andre Homan from the South African rugby union, in *Rugby World Magazine*. 'The growth in merchandising between 1997 [when they were last in South Africa] and 2005 was 3,000% and the growth in the TV audience in the four years between 2001 and 2005 was 20% for the Tests and 110% for the non-Test matches. We're expecting the 2009 visit to generate R1bn [£64m] for the South African economy.'

Professionalism did ensure that some of the Lions traditions were challenged and in 2001 they employed their first overseas coach, New Zealander Graham Henry taking over as they lost 2-1 in Australia. Alongside Henry on that tour, Martin Johnson made history, becoming the first man to captain the Lions on successive tours, after being selected to lead Ian McGeechan's victorious 1997 Lions.

Martin Johnson (right), one of the greatest Lions of them all, with Scott Gibbs, celebrating the 2-1 win in 1997

RECORD BREAKER

STAT ATTACK

John Eales captained Australia a record 55 times, which was more than any other Australian until another legend, George Gregan, surpassed his total.

5 UNFORGETTABLE DAYS

1 JOHN EALES makes a spectacular Wallaby debut as he ruled the lineouts in a 63-6 demolition of Wales in 1991, in his home town of Brisbane, at the famous Ballymore Stadium.

22ND JULY 1991

2 EALES IS a 21-year-old gangly kid in 1991 but that didn't stop him ending the year with a World Cup winner's medal in his pocket, after the 12-6 win over England.

2ND NOV 1991

3 IN THE first 12 seasons of the Tri-Nations, Australia only won it twice, the first time under Eales in 2000, a 24-23 win over New Zealand gained with a last-gasp Eales kick.

5TH AUG 2000

4 EALES JOINED an exclusive club in 1999 when he won his second World Cup, this time as captain, as his side dominated the tournament in Europe, beating France in the final.

6TH NOV 1999

5 EALES'S leadership came to the fore in 2001 when he masterminded the 2-1 series win over the British & Irish Lions, after the Aussies lost the first Test in Brisbane.

14TH JUL 2001

JOHN EALES

Fact file

Full name: John Eales
Date of birth: 27 June, 1970
Place of birth: Brisbane, Australia
Height: 6ft 5in (2m)
Weight: 18st 2lbs (115kg)
Nickname: Nobody
School: Marist College, Ashgrove
Position: Second-row
First cap: 1991 v Wales
Test points: 173
Test caps: 86

AUSTRALIAN LEGEND John Eales was nicknamed 'Nobody' because, as they said of him at the time, 'Nobody's Perfect'.

One of an elite band of players to win two World Cups, in 1991 and 1999, Eales led the Wallabies the second time as they trounced France at the Millennium Stadium, 35-12, after dominating the whole tournament and conceding just one try.

Eales won his reputation because he was a second-row forward who did so much more: kicking goals, marauding around the field like a back-rower, scoring tries and ending up as the highest-scoring forward in the history of the game. Whether as a captain or a skilful second-row, Eales was one of the key reasons why Australia enjoyed the most successful period in their rugby history in the 1990s.

To add to his two World Cup medals, Eales led Australia through three Bledisloe Cup wins, two successful seasons of Tri-Nations fixtures and he was also a key component in the Wallabies first-ever series defeat of the British and Irish Lions, in 2001.

Off the field he became the ultimate sporting ambassador, an Australian with world standing, and it comes as no surprise that the award given to the best Wallaby of the season is called the John Eales Medal.

Revered across the rugby world, Eales retired in 2001 under a weight of tributes, the most significant coming from Australia's Prime Minister John Howard, who said: 'I wish to record my admiration for the magnificent contribution that John Eales has made to the game of rugby, and to Australian and international sport. John Eales has been an inspirational leader, an outstanding and courageous player, and an example to all in the way he has conducted himself.'

> Revered across the rugby world, Eales retired in 2001 under a weight of tributes, the most significant from Prime Minister John Howard.

His talents were quickly translated into the business world and he now works in corporate hospitality and event management. He is also a director of the Sports Australia Hall of Fame and a Fairfax columnist. He was appointed Athlete Liaison Officer for the Australia team at the 2008 Beijing Olympics.

SCOTLAND

RECORD BREAKER

GAVIN HASTINGS

'There is no man more respected for his abilities both on and off the field,' said leading rugby author Clem Thomas.

Fact file

Full name: Andrew Gavin Hastings
Date of birth: 3 May, 1962
Place of birth: Edinburgh, Scotland
Height: 6ft 2in (1.85m)
Weight: 14st 3lbs (88 kg)
Position: Full-back
First cap: 1986 v France
Test caps (Scotland): 61
Test points (Scotland): 667

SCOTTISH RUGBY'S very own Braveheart, Gavin Hastings was one of the best players ever to don the famous dark blue shirt. A graduate of Cambridge University, Hastings broke almost every record Scotland had in his nine-year Test career, also finishing as the leading scorer not just of the Lions but in World Cup history, as he accumulated 227 points in the 1987, 1991 and 1995 Finals.

He retired after the 1995 World Cup with 667 Scotland points to his name, far clear of any other challenger, while his 66 points in Tests for the Lions was the highest ever recorded at the time.

Hastings and Ieuan Evans celebrate the 1989 Lions win

But Hastings was far more than a goalkicker. He was an attacking full-back in the Andy Irvine and JPR Williams mould, his swashbuckling style bringing him 15 Test tries. He captained the 1993 Lions to New Zealand, his credentials established four years earlier when he played in all three Tests as the Lions won 2-1 in Australia.

The Hastings brothers were crucial to that win. In the second Test, Gavin gave them the lead for the first time with fewer than five minutes to play, after a pass from brother Scott.

Gavin also captained Scotland on 20 of his 61 Test appearances, delighted to win his first cap in 1986, alongside Scott...and even more pleased when he kicked all 18 points (a Scottish record) as they won by a point.

But that paled in comparison to his greatest day in a Scotland jersey, when they won the Grand Slam with a final-day victory over England, in 1990, their first clean sweep since 1984.

Chaired off after his last Test match in 1995

STAT ATTACK

Once he retired, Hastings dabbled with a career in American Football, playing for the Scottish Claymores as a kicker, and they won the World Bowl.

5 UNFORGETTABLE DAYS

18TH JAN 1986

1 GAVIN'S Scotland debut against France in 1986 comes alongside brother Scott. Gavin scores all the side's 18 points.

1ST JULY 1989

2 THE HASTINGS brothers make history in Australia in 1989 by becoming the first brothers to appear in the same Lions team.

17TH MAR 1990

3 PERHAPS Gavin's proudest day as he helps Scotland take the biggest prize in European rugby, a Five Nations Grand Slam against England, 13-7.

12TH JUN 1993

4 HASTINGS takes over at the helm of the Lions on their 1993 trip to New Zealand, captaining the side for the first time in the First Test.

11TH JUN 1995

5 GAVIN'S final game for Scotland comes in the 1995 Rugby World Cup. The result doesn't go as Gavin would have liked as Scotland lose 48-30 but they put up a great fight against the All Blacks.

STAT ATTACK
In May 1996 Bath made rugby union history by playing a side from rugby league, the giants of Wigan. The sides played twice, in Manchester under League rules when Wigan won 82-6, and at Twickenham, under union rules when Bath triumphed 44-19.

5 MILESTONES

28TH APR 1984

1 THE FIRST trophy of a staggering run comes at Twickenham as they beat Bristol in the John Player Cup, winning 10-9 under the guidance of new coach, Jack Rowell (left).

14TH MAY 1994

2 NO ONE could touch them in the mid-1990s and in 1994 as they win the League, Cup and Middlesex Sevens titles.

31ST JAN 1998

3 BATH becomes the first English side to lift the prestigious Heineken Cup in 1998 as they beat Brive, 19-18, in a titanic battle in Bordeaux, by virtue of Jon Callard's kicking.

10TH APR 2004

4 BATH almost suffer the unthinkable and are only saved from relegation to National One by points difference.

1ST DEC 2006

5 BATH'S record for developing international coaches continues with Brian Ashton's confirmation as England coach, following former Bath coaches Jack Rowell, Clive Woodward and Andy Robinson into the big job.

ONE OF the greatest clubs in the history of English rugby, Bath were the dominant force in the game as rugby moved from the amateur to the professional era in the 1980s and early 1990s.

Although rugby union finally turned professional in 1995 some of the biggest clubs, like Bath, had been changing attitudes for more than a decade before, and the honours board at the Recreation Ground tells the whole story.

With some of the most innovative rugby thinkers in the game at the time, Bath won the English Cup 10 times and the league title a further six times in a period of domestic dominance between 1984 and 1996 that has never been experienced before or since. Perhaps even more remarkable is the fact that, before that first John Player Cup victory in 1984, which started the run of trophies, Bath had never been past the quarter-finals before!

Their reputation as cup kings preceded them and in 1994, with Jack Rowell as coach, came a unique Grand Slam of titles: the league and cup double were rounded off when Bath lifted the Middlesex Sevens crown, a title which was much-prized in the 1990s.

Bath have developed countless internationals and also successive England coaches; Rowell, Sir Clive Woodward, Andy Robinson and Brian Ashton, all enjoying time at Bath before taking over with England.

One of the oldest clubs in the world, Bath was founded in 1865 and, unlike almost every other club across England, they play their rugby right in the centre of the city, at one of the most picturesque stadiums you could imagine.

In the fully professional era Bath, now owned by greeting card magnate Andrew Brownsword, failed to maintain their high standards. Although they were crowned the best side in Europe in 1998, winning the Heineken Cup, they had to wait until 2008 for the next trophy, when they won the European Challenge Cup.

Quick stats

NAME: Bath Rugby **FOUNDED:** 1865
STADIUM: The Recreation Ground
COLOURS: Blue, Black and White
COACH: Steve Meehan
HONOURS: Heineken Cup winners: 1998. English League: 1989, 1991, 1992, 1993, 1994, 1996. English Cup: 1984, 1985, 1986, 1987, 1989, 1990, 1992, 1994, 1995, 1996

www.bathrugby.com

3 GREAT PLAYERS

1. JEREMY GUSCOTT: The prince of centres, Guscott cut a swathe through defences in the 1980s and 1990s as he ruled supreme for Bath, England and the British & Irish Lions. Embodied the Bath style of fast, free-flowing rugby.

2. ROGER SPURRELL: A fearsome back-row forward who came to prominence in their great sides of the 1980s, Spurrell did a great job winning the ball. Scored a crucial try in the 1986 cup final as Bath roared back from being behind to beat Wasps.

3. ANDY ROBINSON: One of a select band of Bath players to go on and coach the side, Andy Robinson was part of the 1998 Heineken Cup-winning team. After his retirement, he became Bath's Director of Rugby and soon England's second-in- command under Clive Woodward. Robinson took over as England coach in 2004, only lasting two years in the job, before being sacked and replaced by another Bath man in Brian Ashton.

Quick stats

NAME: The Brumbies
FOUNDED: 1938
STADIUM: Canberra Stadium
COLOURS: White, Blue and Yellow
COACH: Andy Friend
HONOURS: Super 12 winners: 2001 and 2004.

www.brumbies.com.au

IF IT WASN'T for the ACT (Australia Capital Territory) Brumbies, teams from New Zealand would have won every one of the first 12 titles in the history of the Super 12. But the Brumbies produced a golden generation of players at the end of the 1990s that led to triumphs in 2000 and 2001. Known today only as a Super 14 franchise, the ACT has a long and rich history dating back to 1938 when the state fielded their first representative side against the All Blacks during their nine-match undefeated tour of Australia.

As a side they played sporadically over the years and it wasn't until the establishment of the Super 12 in 1996 that the ACT Brumbies (now known just as the Brumbies) began to get regular competition.

Even though the Brumbies only tended to play touring sides in the early years, it didn't stop them picking up a number of notable victories, including victories over Wales and Tonga in the 1970s.

But it was with the birth of the Super 12 that the ACT side gained world notoriety. In the early years of the Super 12 they were lucky to be guided by two visionary coaches, Rod Macqueen and Eddie Jones, both of whom went on to take charge of Australia.

A defeat in the 1997 final showed their intentions and, with the Wallabies side littered with Brumbies like George Gregan, George Smith and Joe Roff, they took the title in both 2001 and 2004, the second time in one of the greatest finals in the competition's history.

DID YOU KNOW?
In 2004 the territory of the ACT Rugby Union was expanded to incorporate the Far South Coast and Southern Inland Unions. The ACT Rugby Union was renamed the 'ACT and Southern NSW Rugby Union'. The team name was changed to Brumbies Rugby.

5 MILESTONES

1 THE ACT union is formed just before the Second World War, with University, Easts, RMS and Norths forming the sides in the inaugural competition.

1938

2 THE ACT's first international victory comes in 1973 when they beat Tonga 17-6, a notable win as the Tongans go on to inflict a humiliating defeat on Australia.

1973

3 THE MOST memorable win in the history of the ACT side comes against the Grand Slam champions of Wales in 1978, conquerors of all that Europe could muster.

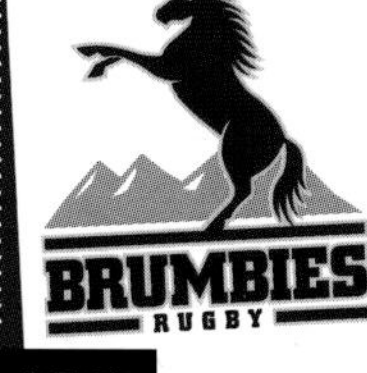

1978

4 AT THE turn of the century the Brumbies, under Eddie Jones, became the first non-New Zealand side to win the Super 12, as they beat the Sharks from SA, 51-10.

26 MAY 2001

5 SUPER 12 title one becomes number two in 2004 as new coach David Nucifora guides them to a spectacular 47-38 final victory over the Crusaders at Canberra Stadium.

23RD MAY 2004

BIGGEST WIN

The Brumbies have handed out 64-point hammerings twice in their history, beating the Cats 64-0 in 2001 and the Bulls 79-15 in 1999.

3 GREAT PLAYERS

1. GEORGE GREGAN: The scrum-half extraordinaire who won a record 137 Test caps was a key part of the Brumbies' two victories in the Super 12. Sniping at the base of the scrum, Gregan embodied the team spirit of the Brumbies, a side that included many New South Wales rejects. His underdog attitude was the cornerstone for their amazing success.

2. STIRLING MORTLOCK: No player has scored more points in a career or in a season (194 in 2000) than the Brumbies centre who has been a superior attacking threat both in the Super 12 and when he has been on Australia duty. He captained the side to their Super 12 success in 2004, as they took the tournament by storm.

3. JOE ROFF: The Brumbies wing scored an incredible 57 tries in his eight-season career (1996-2004) and even bagged 15 in one campaign (1997) as he lit up the Super 12. A maverick in the best sense of the word, he also had a spell at Biarritz, finishing his career captaining Oxford in the Varsity Match.

5 MILESTONES

30TH MAY 1998

1 BOTTOM OF the pile in 1996, the Crusaders turn things around in spectacular style to win the Super 12 in 1998 with a final win over Auckland, 20-13.

29TH MAY 1999

2 NO SECOND-season syndrome for the Crusaders as they back up their first win in 1998 with another crown.

28TH MAY 2000

3 WITH WAYNE Smith off to coach at the All Blacks how would they fare? Business as usual with another title, beating George Gregan's Brumbies.

25TH MAY 2002

4 THE 2001 season sees them drop to 10th in the table but they roared back in 2002, to beat the Brumbies.

27TH MAY 2006

5 TWO MORE teams in the competition make it the Super 14, but the Crusaders don't break their stride, winning their sixth title with a victory in the final over the Waratahs.

DID YOU KNOW?
Before every match the Crusaders' supporters are 'whipped into a frenzy' by eight horses and riders from the Christchurch Polo Club, who are dressed up like knights from the medieval times, circling the pitch. The tradition dates back to the first settlers in the 1800s.

THE MOST successful side in the history of Super rugby, the Crusaders (formerly Canterbury Crusaders) came to the fore in the mid-1990s and have stayed at the top of their game.

Like all the sides in the Super 14, the Crusaders are a franchise but in the case of the men in red and black this franchise is backed by a history of magnificent rugby under the Canterbury banner.

The Canterbury Rugby Union was formed in 1879, incorporating the seven provinces in the top half of the South Island of New Zealand, playing a lot of its rugby in Canterbury, a city largely of English origin.

By the end of the 2008 season the Crusaders had won the Super 12 and 14 a record seven times, but they haven't always dominated the new southern hemisphere tournament. They actually finished last in the inaugural competition in 1996.

But a top-to-bottom review of the region saw a rugby revolution that was reflected in the selection of the New Zealand team. In five years, the Crusaders went from being a largely non-All Blacks environment, with just one player in the team, to having all but one of the All Blacks when 14 Crusaders lined up for New Zealand in the starting line-up against Ireland in 2002.

The revolution was helped by some innovative coaching first from current All Blacks backs coach Wayne Smith, from 1997 to 1999, and later his successor Robbie Deans, who was named coach of Australia in 2008. Both men are former Canterbury players.

The breakthrough came with a hat-trick of Super 12 titles from 1998 to 2000.

Under Deans' control, the Crusaders only once failed to make the Super rugby final, winning more titles in 2002, 2005 and 2006, while finishing as runners-up in 2003 and 2004, setting a new standard for the competition and giving a benchmark for every side to aspire to.

In 2008 they captured their seventh title, beating the Waratahs, 20-12.

CRUSADERS

Quick stats

NAME: The Crusaders
FOUNDED: 1879
STADIUM: Lancaster Park
COLOURS: Red and Black
HONOURS: Super 12 winners: 1998, 1999, 2000, 2002, 2005. Super 14 winners: 2006, 2008

www.crusaders.co.nz

STAT ATTACK
In 2007, the Crusaders became the first side in the history of Super rugby to win 100 matches, when they inflicted a 53-0 defeat on the Force.

▼THREE GREAT PLAYERS

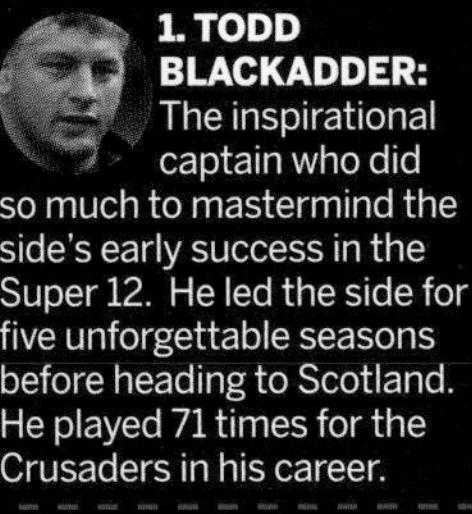

1. TODD BLACKADDER: The inspirational captain who did so much to mastermind the side's early success in the Super 12. He led the side for five unforgettable seasons before heading to Scotland. He played 71 times for the Crusaders in his career.

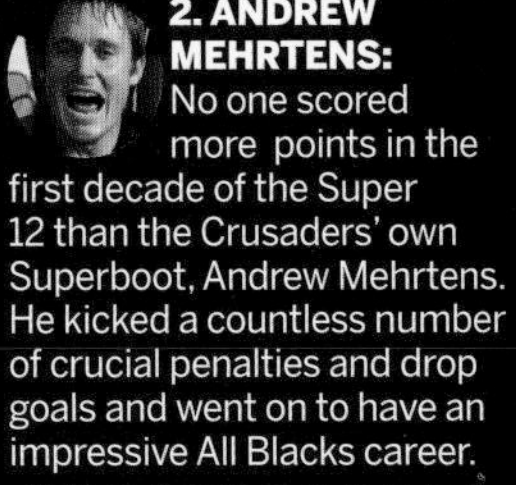

2. ANDREW MEHRTENS: No one scored more points in the first decade of the Super 12 than the Crusaders' own Superboot, Andrew Mehrtens. He kicked a countless number of crucial penalties and drop goals and went on to have an impressive All Blacks career.

3. RICHIE McCAW: Another great leader who built on the success of Blackadder and captained the side to titles in 2005, 2006 and 2008. A supreme competitor at the breakdown, McCaw took his skills on to the All Blacks as they set standards across the world.

Quick stats

NAME: Leicester Football Club
FOUNDED: 1880
STADIUM: Welford Road
COLOURS: Green, White and Red
COACH: Marcelo Loffreda
HONOURS: Heineken Cup winners: 2001, 2002, English League: 1988, 1995, 1999, 2000, 2001, 2002, 2007 English Cup: 1979, 80, 81, 93, 97 & 07.

www.leicestertigers.com

ONE OF the standard bearers for English rugby in the professional era, Leicester Tigers have stood like a colossus over the domestic scene since the game ditched its amateur history after the World Cup in 1995.

Formed in 1880 as an amalgamation of three separate clubs, Leicester Alert, Leicester Amateur FC, and the Leicester Societies AFC, five years later they added the Tigers name.

Leagues started in England in 1987 and, although Leicester won it in its second season and again in 1995, it took until the turn of the century for the United Kingdom's best-supported club to take an iron grip on the game in England, by winning four successive titles from 1999 to 2002, also becoming the first team to win back-to-back Heineken Cups.

One of only four sides never to have been relegated from the top division, Leicester have never finished lower than sixth.

Their trophy-laden recent history was underpinned by their form at Welford Road: between December 1997 and November 2002 they went 57 games unbeaten at home.

In 2008 Leicester failed in their bid to win any silverware, losing in the final of the EDF Energy Cup to the Ospreys, and losing in the Guinness Premiership final to London Wasps.

In 2008 they confirmed plans to build the biggest rugby-only club ground in the United Kingdom, with a capacity of 23,500.

STAT ATTACK
Leicester Tigers' transformation in just over 30 years has been incredible. At the start of the 1970s they had gates of around 1,000 but by 2008 that had grown to an average of 17,000 for a club that now has an annual turnover of a staggering £15 million.

5 MILESTONES

1 THE NATIONAL Cup kicks off in 1972 and it isn't long before Leicester are taking the trophy, as they beat Moseley in 1979 with 11 points from kicker Dusty Hare (below).

21ST APR 1979

2 IT TOOK four years to arrive but Leicester finally break their duck in the professional era, winning the first of four English titles, under the coaching of Dean Richards.

16TH MAY 1999

3 ONLY ONE English club had won the European Cup before 1999 but in 2002 Leicester complete back-to-back titles, confirming them as the best rugby team in Europe.

27TH MAY 2002

4 UNDER COACH Dean Richards and inspirational captain Martin Johnson, Leicester win their fourth successive English league title, a truly remarkable achievement.

13TH APR 2002

5 THEY WIN their first piece of silverware for five years lifting the EDF Energy Cup, beating the Ospreys 41-35 with tries from Tom Varndell, Tom Croft, Ben Kay and Alesana Tuilagi.

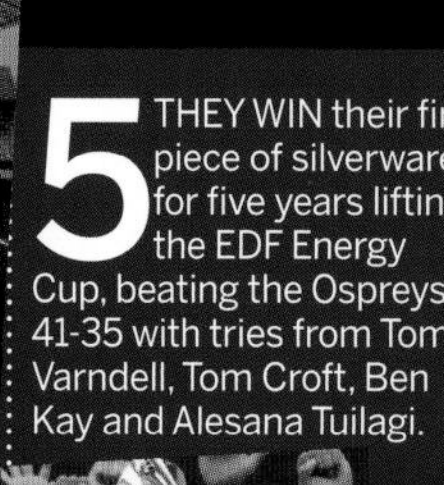

15TH APR 2007

3 GREAT PLAYERS

1. MARTIN JOHNSON CBE: Perhaps the greatest player in the history of the game learnt his trade at Leicester, after spells at Wigston and in New Zealand. A three-time British and Irish Lion, Johnson was Leicester captain when they won four successive English championships and back-to-back Heineken Cup finals at the turn of the century. Formidable at lineout time, Johnson was an uncompromising defender and a leader without comparison in the history of English rugby.

2. RORY UNDERWOOD: The Leicester flyer scored more tries (49) for England than anyone in the history of the game and was a similarly unstoppable force in the green, red and white of the Leicester Tigers.

3. GRAHAM ROWNTREE: The most decorated member of the famous Leicester ABC Club, so called because in the amateur days the players used to wear letters on their backs, rather than numbers, the first three in the alphabet signifying the Tigers front-row forwards.

LLANELLi SCARLETS

THE LLANELLI Scarlets were born in 2004 when the Welsh Rugby Union made the decision to abandon their traditional clubs in the professional era, instead establishing four regional (or provincial) sides to play in the Magners League, Heineken Cup and EDF Energy (Anglo-Welsh) Cup.

The Scarlets joined the Ospreys, Newport Gwent Dragons, the Cardiff Blues and the Celtic Warriors, who were to fold, leaving just four Welsh sides in the cross-border competitions.

This meant that Llanelli Scarlets were no longer just representing the town of Llanelli but a far bigger geographical area, which even encompasses North Wales.

The beginning of the Llanelli Scarlets should always be seen as a rebirth, as they represent more than 120 years of rugby history, one of the most famous clubs in the world.

Llanelli have been Wales' most successful side in the Heineken Cup. Even though Cardiff reached one final, Llanelli's consistency sets them apart, making quarter-finals and semi-finals on a regular basis. And they also recorded some great victories against tourists, the most notable being the 9-3 win over New Zealand in 1972 when 'the pubs ran dry'.

The region, and Llanelli RFC, who play in the Welsh Premier Division, have decided to leave their famous home at Stradey Park, where they have played since 1879, for a £45 million, 13,000 all-seater stadium at nearby Pemberton.

Quick stats

NAME: Llanelli Scarlets
FOUNDED: 1872
STADIUM: Stradey Park
COLOURS: Red and White
COACH: Phil Davies
HONOURS: Welsh Cup: 1973, 1974, 1975, 1976, 1985, 1988, 1991, 1992, 1993, 1998, 2000, 2003, 2005. Celtic League: 2004

www.scarlets.co.uk

DID YOU KNOW?

They haven't always worn their famous red jerseys. According to the club's official history the first Llanelli colours were dark blue with high collared jerseys and tight trousers reaching well below the knee. The first real match was against Cambrian Club, in January 1876.

▼5 MILESTONES

1 IN WEST Wales they still talk of the day when Llanelli beat the All Blacks, at the famous Stradey Park, 9-3. Coached by Carwyn James, Roy Bergiers scored the only try.

31ST OCT 1972

2 ANOTHER GREAT day for the men from west Wales as they beat the Australian tourists 13-9 at Stradey Park, Ieuan Evans (above) getting the winning try.

14TH NOV 1992

3 LLANELLI WIN the WRU Heineken League in 1993 and are named the Best Team in Britain after an incredible year that also saw them lift the WRU Challenge Cup.

8TH MAY 1993

4 LLANELLI'S FIRST Heineken Cup semi-final comes in 2000, but they lose (31-28) to a Paul Grayson injury-time penalty against Northampton, the eventual Cup winners.

6TH MAY 2000

5 THE FIRST season of regional rugby brings the Scarlets the Celtic League title, four points ahead of Ulster after they rack up 16 wins from their 22 games, scoring almost 600 points.

14TH MAY 2004

DID YOU KNOW?

Sospan Fach (little saucepan) is a famous Welsh song, which reverberates around Stradey Park, and there are saucepans on top of the posts at Stradey.

3 GREAT PLAYERS

1. RAY GRAVELL: The centre from Burry Port embodied the club for decades, playing in the famous win over New Zealand in 1972 and going on to skipper the side for two years. A Wales regular, Gravell went on to enjoy a career in broadcasting and acting before sadly dying in 2007, a full house packing into Stradey for his memorial service.

2. PHIL BENNETT: The king of the sidestep, Phil Bennett started the move that led to rugby's most famous try when the Barbarians played New Zealand in 1973. But it is in the colours of his beloved Llanelli that he made his name and where he played for 16 great seasons.

3. SCOTT QUINNELL: A member of the most famous rugby dynasty in Welsh rugby, perhaps the world, Scott followed father Derek and uncle Barry (John) into the Welsh team and was himself joined by brother Craig. He played rugby league at the highest level and had a spell at Richmond when they were flying high but returned to Stradey to help them to the 2004 Celtic League title.

DID YOU KNOW?

Munster's 1978 win over New Zealand inspired a play; *Alone it Stands* by John Breen, and a book called *Stand Up and Fight* by Alan English.

5 MILESTONES

1 WINS OVER the All Blacks are rare but in 1978 Munster become the only Irish side ever to beat them, winning 12-0 in a match where Tony Ward kicked two drop goals.

31ST OCT 1978

2 MUNSTER'S first Heineken Cup final appearance comes in 2000 when they lose by a point to Northampton.

27TH MAY 2000

3 THEY GO into their final group game in 2003 against Gloucester needing to win by at least 27 points and score a minimum of four tries...and incredibly they do it!

18TH JAN 2003

4 FINALLY... The Heineken Cup win they craved comes with a victory over Biarritz. European champions at last!

20TH MAY 2006

5 A TRY from Denis Leamy (left) and the boot of Ronan O'Gara brought Munster their second Heineken Cup victory, this time 16-13 over Toulouse, at the Millennium Stadium.

24TH MAY 2008

STAT ATTACK

Munster hold one rather bizarre record. Due to their large numbers of travelling fans they ensured the highest ever attendance, of 32,000, for a rugby match in Spain, set when they played Biarritz in 2005, the French club deciding to move the tie across the border to San Sebastián.

THE IRISH province with the country's best record in European competition, Munster have flown the flag in successive Heineken Cup campaigns and have been the only side from the country to beat the famous New Zealand All Blacks.

Consistent performances in Europe, since the Heineken Cup kick-off in 1995, built on a successful history, which until that point had reached its pinnacle in 1978 when they beat the All Blacks.

That 12-0 win over New Zealand in Limerick, with points from Tony Ward and Christy Cantillon, followed up a draw with the same side in 1973.

In Europe, Munster became the force they are today in the late 1990s. They had a series of near-misses, making it to the final in 2000 and 2002, but finally lifted the trophy in 2006 in a pulsating final against Biarritz at the Millennium Stadium.

A 74,500-strong sell-out crowd packed into Cardiff in 2006 (as many as 50,000 were supporting Munster!), with thousands more watching the game in the streets of Limerick and Cork. All were enthralled by a great performance from their side which saw tries coming from Peter Stringer and Trevor Halstead, and 13 points from Ronan O'Gara.

One of the best-supported rugby teams on the planet, Munster regularly pack out their Thomond Park ground and thousands will follow the team around Europe.

Those supporters ensured that Munster were part of the most-attended quarter-final (v Perpignan, 49,500 in 2006) and semi-final (v Wasps, 49,500 in 2004).

In 2008 Munster capped an incredible season by winning the Heineken Cup, beating Toulouse 16-13 in the final in Cardiff.

Munster is, of course, more than just a senior rugby team; it is a rugby union, encompassing 15 domestic teams, including Shannon, Garryowen and Cork Constitution, and a number of provincial competitions.

It is a branch of the Irish Rugby Football Union, having a different and much closer relationship with their governing body than the clubs in England. Formed in 1879, the branch has always played rugby under its own banner.

Munster have big plans for the future, transforming their famous, but slightly dilapidated, Thomond Park home into a 26,000-capacity stadium at the cost of €40 million.

Quick stats

NAME: Munster
FOUNDED: 1879
STADIUMS: Thomond Park and Musgrave Park
COLOURS: Red, Navy and White
HONOURS: Heineken Cup: 2006 and 2008. Celtic League: 2003. Celtic Cup: 2005.

www.munsterrugby.ie

▼THREE GREAT PLAYERS

1. KEITH WOOD: The 'flying potato' is renowned as one of the greatest hookers of the modern era, starring for Munster, Harlequins and captaining Ireland more times than any player before him. His strength was in his leadership and work around the park that brought 15 tries in his 58 Tests for Ireland.

2. RONAN O'GARA: A deadly right boot and an astute tactical brain puts the Munster outside-half in the league of legends. USA-born O'Gara has set records for his province and Ireland in a great career, and by the end of the 2008 Six Nations he had scored 827 Test points.

3. PAUL O'CONNELL: A fearsome second-row operator, Paul O'Connell scored a try on his Test debut in 2002 against Wales and has never looked back. A Lion in 2005, Limerick-born O'Connell is as much of a threat around the field as he is at lineout time.

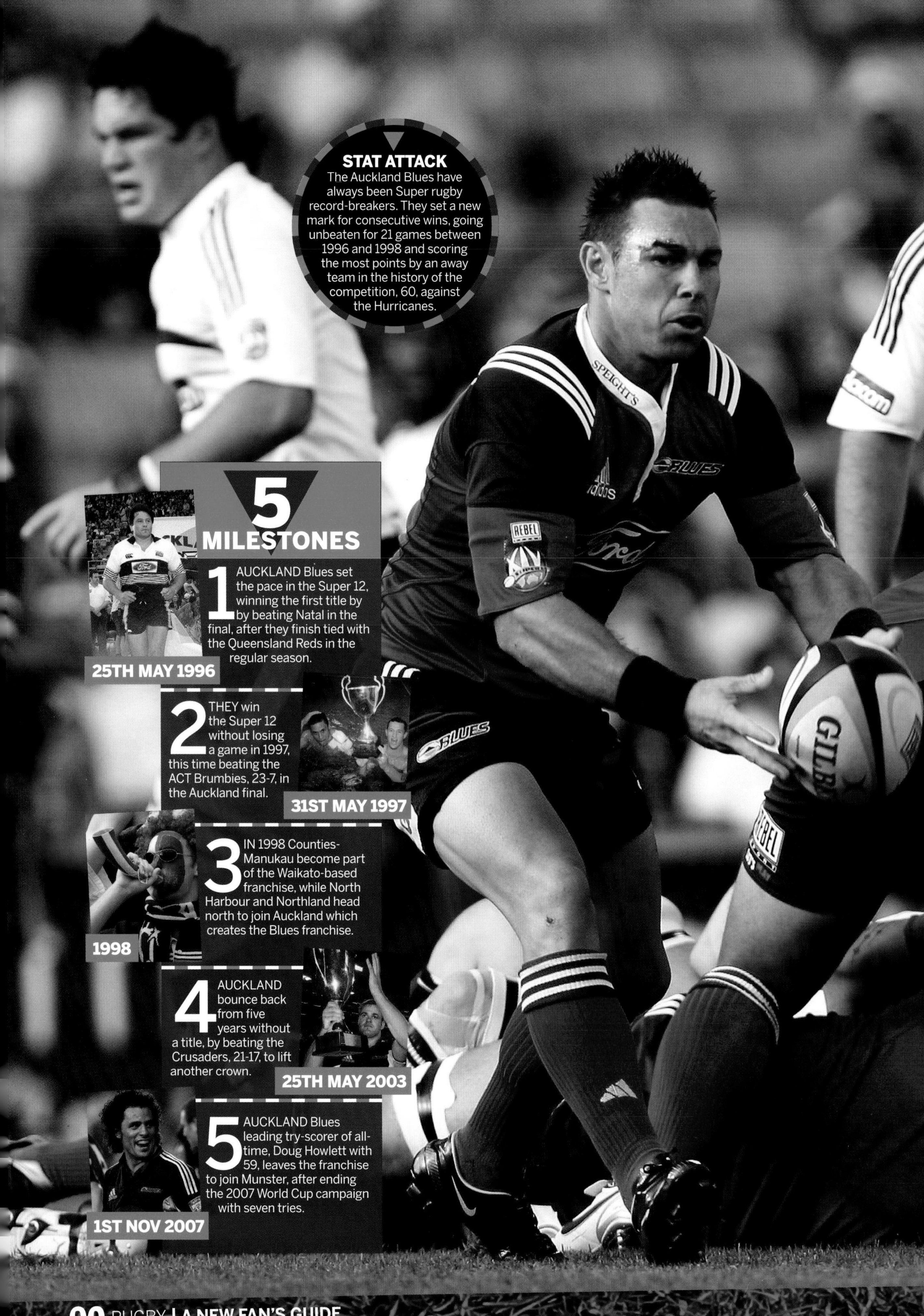

STAT ATTACK
The Auckland Blues have always been Super rugby record-breakers. They set a new mark for consecutive wins, going unbeaten for 21 games between 1996 and 1998 and scoring the most points by an away team in the history of the competition, 60, against the Hurricanes.

5 MILESTONES

1 AUCKLAND Blues set the pace in the Super 12, winning the first title by by beating Natal in the final, after they finish tied with the Queensland Reds in the regular season.

25TH MAY 1996

2 THEY win the Super 12 without losing a game in 1997, this time beating the ACT Brumbies, 23-7, in the Auckland final.

31ST MAY 1997

3 IN 1998 Counties-Manukau become part of the Waikato-based franchise, while North Harbour and Northland head north to join Auckland which creates the Blues franchise.

1998

4 AUCKLAND bounce back from five years without a title, by beating the Crusaders, 21-17, to lift another crown.

25TH MAY 2003

5 AUCKLAND Blues leading try-scorer of all-time, Doug Howlett with 59, leaves the franchise to join Munster, after ending the 2007 World Cup campaign with seven tries.

1ST NOV 2007

DID YOU KNOW?

The Blues have their roots in the Auckland Rugby Union, which was founded in 1883, the regional identifiers being dropped in 2000.

WHEN RUGBY turned professional in 1995, the Auckland Blues (later to become the Blues) were one of the quickest sides out of the blocks, dominating the early years of the Super 12 competition, leaning heavily on a golden generation of players.

Kicking off the Super 12, Auckland Blues, representing the Northland, North Harbour and Auckland unions, won the first two competitions, in 1996 and 1997, making it a hat-trick of titles in 2003. Auckland were guided to their first two crowns by Graham Henry, the coach who went on to take charge of Wales, the Lions and New Zealand.

The first title in 1996 was won with a final victory over Natal, 46-22, at Eden Park, and the second, won 23-7 against ACT Brumbies, followed in a season of complete domination as The Auckland Blues completed the season without losing a game.

In the first two seasons Auckland Blues' side was littered with stars, from Sean Fitzpatrick in the front row to Zinzan Brooke in the back row, and the deadly 'Double Js' combination on the wings of Joeli Vidiri and the incomparable Jonah Lomu, both men scoring in the first final. The boot of Adrian Cashmore was also crucial in those early years as he cashed in with vital points in the first two finals.

In 2003, the Blues – who lost to Canterbury Crusaders in the 1998 final – gained revenge, becoming Super 12 champions again, 21-17.

With the expansion of the franchise system the Auckland Blues, along with the other New Zealand teams, dropped their geographical monicker to be known simply as the Blues.

In 2008, the Blues endured a disappointing campaign finishing sixth, even though they went to the top of the table at the start of March after scoring seven tries for the second consecutive game to defeat Central Cheetahs 50-26.

Quick stats

NAME: The Blues (Auckland)
FOUNDED: 1880
STADIUM: Eden Park
COLOURS: Blue
COACH: David Nucifora
HONOURS: Super 12 winners: 1996, 1997 and 2003

www.theblues.co.nz

3 GREAT PLAYERS

1. SEAN FITZPATRICK: One of the greatest hookers in the history of the game, Fitzpatrick played a then world record 92 times for New Zealand. Even though Fitzy had some of his best rugby behind him when the Super 12 was launched, he was still able to be a key reason for Auckland's triumph in the competition's first year.

2. JONAH LOMU: The giant wing man was unstoppable in Test rugby so at Super 12 he ran amok, especially in the competition's first year (1996) when he scored in the final. He went on to play for Waikato Chiefs, and the Hurricanes.

3. MICHAEL JONES: Perhaps the greatest All Black in history, Jones, who was of Samoan heritage, was an openside flanker of the highest order, gracing the early years of the Super 12. Auckland coach John Hart described Jones as "almost the perfect player", only a series of injuries preventing him winning more than 55 caps. Jones went on to coach Samoa at the 2007 World Cup.

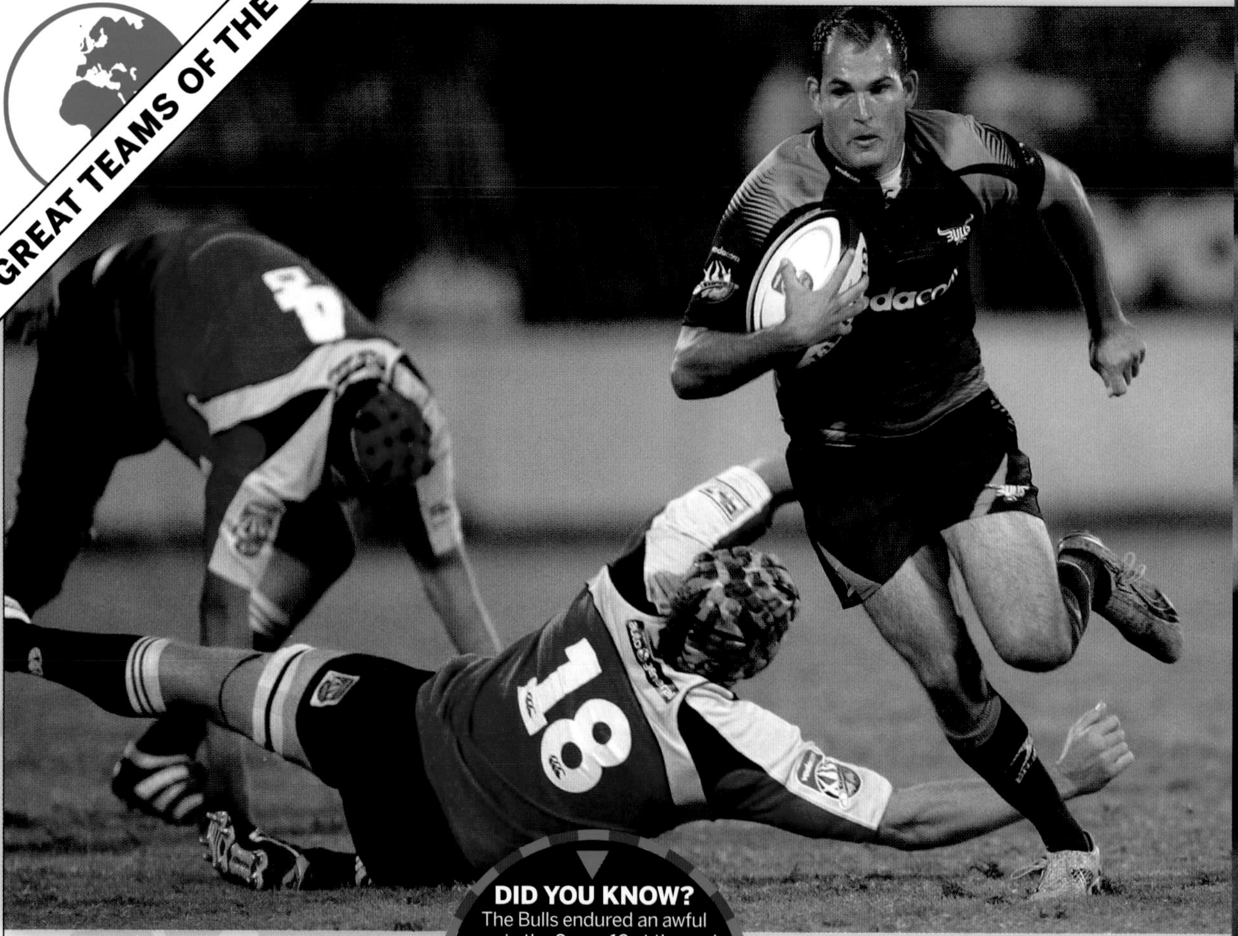

DID YOU KNOW?
The Bulls endured an awful run in the Super 12 at the end of the 1990s, finishing last three times and 11th twice between 1998 and 2002, only turning the corner in 2003 when they finished a far more respectable sixth. The 2002 season was the worst when they failed to win a game.

IT TOOK 12 years for a South African side to end the duopoly that the New Zealand and Australian sides had enforced on the Super 12, but when the breakthrough came in 2007 it came in style with the Bulls beating the Sharks in an epic final.

The Pretoria-based franchise and their Shark-infested neighbours from Durban set the tone for a magnificent year for the country as they ended the season with South Africa as world champions.

Wing Bryan Habana had the final say in that 2007 final, scoring a last-minute try, converted by Derick Hougaard, to win the game 20-19 for the Pretoria-based side. It is difficult to overestimate how important the form of the Bulls and the Sharks was in laying the foundation for the World Cup victory later that year.

The Bulls, who were captained in 2007 by Springboks scrum-half Fourie du Preez, draw most of their players from the Blue Bulls (Pretoria plus Limpopo Province), who play in the Currie Cup, but can also use men from the Falcons (East Rand).

The current Bulls actually started out life in the first Super 12 competition in 1996 as the Blue Bulls, as South Africa allowed their top Currie Cup teams to represent them.

Until they won the competition in 2007, their best performance had been in the inaugural competition, when they finished third in the table, losing to Auckland Blues in the semi-finals.

They play at the famous Loftus Versfeld stadium in Pretoria, which is also used by the Blue Bulls. They were pioneers in tournaments with Australia and New Zealand under the monicker of Northern Transvaal, having been part of the Super 10 in 1993.

Quick stats

NAME: The Bulls
FOUNDED: 1997
STADIUM: Loftus Versfeld
COLOURS: Blue and Black
COACH: Frans Ludeke
HONOURS: Super 14 winners: 2007.

www.thebulls.co.za

STAT ATTACK

Louis Koen had an incredible Super 12 season in 2003, kicking a record seven drop goals for the franchise, three of them coming in one game against the Cats.

3 GREAT PLAYERS

1. JOOST VAN DER WESTHUIZEN: One of the greatest scrum-halves in the history of the game, Joost ended his career with a recordn 89 South Africa caps, and with 38 tries more than any No 9 from any country. A game-breaker, he was deadly around the base of the scrum and ruck. A World Cup winner in 1995, he retired from Tests in 2003.

2. VICTOR MATFIELD: The man of the match in the 2007 World Cup final, Matfield has been an outstanding international player, and a great servant of the Bulls, since his South Africa debut in 2001. Widely regarded as the best lock of his era.

3. BRYAN HABANA: One of the quickest and most elusive wings the game has seen, Habana's try won the 2007 Super 14 and he ended the year scoring a record-equalling eight tries at the World Cup as South Africa lifted the Webb Ellis Cup, at the Stade de France.

5 MILESTONES

1 AS NORTHERN Transvaal they finish third in the first Super 12 competition, only to lose to the eventual winners, Auckland Blues, in the semi-finals, 48-11.

19TH MAY 1996

2 MORNE STEYN sets a record for points in a match for the Bulls in 2005 when he scores an incredible 35 against the Stormers, when the Bulls finish a creditable third.

14TH MAY 2005

3 FOR THE second year running the Bulls are the only South African side in the top four of the Super 12. This time though they go out to eventual winners, the Crusaders.

20TH MAY 2006

4 IF ANYONE doubts the Super 14 credentials of the Bulls, the worries are removed when they smash the Queensland Reds by an incredible, record, 92-3.

5TH MAY 2007

5 IT TOOK 12 seasons but when a South African winner of the Super competition comes it is the Bulls, as they win an all-South African final against the Sharks.

19TH MAY 2007

DID YOU KNOW?

Toulouse coach Guy Noves is one of the longest serving bosses in Europe, taking over at the helm of the French giants in 1992, and leading them to glory.

5 MILESTONES

1 IN THE MIDDLE of a great domestic run it is no surprise that Toulouse make the first Heineken Cup final, beating Cardiff at the Arms Park, 21-18.

7TH JAN 1996

2 AN ALL-French European final in Dublin sees Toulouse beat Perpignan 22-17, after they build up a 19-point half-time lead.

24TH MAY 2003

3 TOULOUSE are part of the biggest game, in attendance terms, ever in the French Championship as an incredible 79,502 watch them take on Stade Français.

30TH APR 2005

4 THE TENTH anniversary Heineken Cup final sees Toulouse complete the hat-trick with a win over Stade Français.

22ND MAY 2005

5 SO CLOSE but yet so far for the artisans of European rugby. In 2008 they were pipped by Munster, losing 16-13, as they went for their fourth Heineken Cup title.

24TH MAY 2008

THE MANCHESTER United of French rugby, Toulouse set the standards in European rugby as the first side to win three Heineken Cups.

The leading French side in European rugby, the club known in their homeland as Stade Toulousain, again made the final in 2008 although this time they came up just short, losing 16-13, in a titanic battle with Munster in Cardiff.

They have a history of success in France that stretches back to the start of the last century, when the club also had a vibrant soccer team that lifted a number of regional championships. Founded in 1890, the rugby side of the club won their first French title in 1912 and took five more in the 1920s.

The glory years almost completely deserted the club until they came to be one of the dominant forces in French rugby in the 1980s and 1990s, taking the advent of professionalism in their stride and allowing the new era of rugby to make the club even stronger.

The pinnacle of this domination came in the mid-1990s, under inspirational coach Guy Noves, when they claimed four French titles in a row and also picked up the Heineken Cup, soon becoming the first side to become European champions three times.

Toulouse, with Emile Ntamack as captain, won the first Heineken Cup, at the famous Cardiff Arms Park in 1996, in front of 21,800 fans, requiring extra time before beating Cardiff 21-18, and kicking off their time at the top of European rugby.

For some of their bigger games, they use the Stade de Toulouse, a multi-use stadium in the city, rather than the Stade Ernest-Wallon. Stade de Toulouse is used mostly for football matches, by Toulouse FC. The stadium is able to hold 37,000.

STAT ATTACK

Toulouse became the first side in the history of the Heineken Cup to score 100 points in a match, hammering Ebbw Vale 108-16 in the 1998-99 season. The huge scoreline allowed them to set another record with the most tries (16) ever scored in one match.

Quick stats

NAME: Stade Toulousain
FOUNDED: 1890
STADIUM: Stade Ernest-Wallon
COLOURS: Red and Black
COACH: Guy Noves
HONOURS: Heineken Cup winners: 1996, 2003, 2005, French League: 1912, 1922, 1923, 1924, 1926, 1927, 1947, 1985, 1986, 1989, 1994, 1995, 1996, 1997, 1999, 2001. French Cup: 1946, 1947, 1984.

www.stadetoulousain.net

3 GREAT PLAYERS

1. EMILE NTAMACK: A huge figure in French rugby in the 1990s, he was at the centre of much of Toulouse's domination of the domestic scene in that decade. Part of France's Grand Slam-winning side in 1997, he became part of the France coaching set-up in 2008 when Marc Lievremont took over the top job in the country.

2. JEAN-PIERRE RIVES: The blond bombshell was in the ascendancy in the era (1970s) when the France team was in a ding-dong battle with Wales for the right to call themselves the best side in Europe. He won two Grand Slams in 1977 and 1981 and was the country's player of the year on three occasions.

3. FABIEN PELOUS: The most capped Frenchman in the history of the game, the giant lock had represented his country a staggering 118 times when he retired at the end of the 2007 World Cup, enjoying a 12-year Test career when he made the France second-row position his own.

BIGGEST WIN

The biggest win in Wasps' history came in 1998 when they hammered West Hartlepool 71-14, scoring ten tries against the side from the north east.

IT TOOK WASPS until 1986 to make the first cup final in their history but, when professionalism arrived in the game a decade later, they quickly became one of the two (alongside Leicester) most successful clubs in England.

They should have been founder members of the Rugby Football Union (RFU), as Wasps were founded after a split from the Harlequins in 1867, four years before the RFU was formed. But a mix-up saw then-president James Pain miss the vital meeting, and so they lost out on their chance to become part of rugby's history.

Wasps have suffered a nomadic existence in recent years as their famous Sudbury ground simply wasn't up to the rigours of the modern game. They first landed at Loftus Road, in a groundshare with Queen's Park Rangers but, when that ended in 2002, they were forced to decamp out of London and share a ground with Wycombe Wanderers FC, a move which has turned into an unexpected success for the club. They adopted their name of London Wasps just before their latest move, as if to reinforce their historical place in the capital city.

They are a club that loves to buck the trend and the phrase 'Once a Wasp, always a Wasp' sums up the team spirit and sporting ethic that has seen them upset so many of the so-called 'bigger clubs' in the modern era of professional rugby.

Their success has brought them a long line of trophies, becoming European champions twice, in 2004 and 2007, when they beat Leicester in the final at Twickenham.

A year later, in 2008, they were back at Twickenham, again beating Leicester in the Guinness Premiership final, in Lawrence Dallaglio's last game as a Wasp.

Quick stats

NAME: London Wasps RFC
FOUNDED: 1867
STADIUM: Adams Park
COLOURS: Black and Gold
COACH: Ian McGeechan
HONOURS: Heineken Cup winners: 2004, 2007, English League: 1990, 1997, 2003, 2004, 2005, 2008. English Cup: 1989, 2000 and 2006

www.wasps.co.uk

3 GREAT PLAYERS

1. LAWRENCE DALLAGLIO: The heart and soul of the club in the professional era, Dallaglio arrived at Sudbury as a teenager and despite many offers played the whole of his career at Wasps. He became club captain in 1995 and was at the helm as Wasps secured a series of trophies in the decade (and more) that followed, winning every domestic and international honour the game has to offer.

2. ROB ANDREW: After graduating from Cambridge, Andrew's almost unerring right boot took him into legendary status at the club as they won the Courage League in 1990.

3. RICHARD SHARP: One of the first players to be inducted into the Wasps Hall of Fame, Sharp was credited with scoring one of the greatest tries in England's history against Scotland in 1963 as he captained his country to the Five Nations title. He made his Wasps debut in 1957, following father Freddie and uncle Ivan.

5 MILESTONES

1 AS ENGLAND delay the onset of true professionalism until 1996, Wasps win the first League title in the new era, joining Leicester and Bath as the only champions in the decade.

26TH APR 1997

2 WASPS MAKE a crucial move to their new home at Wycombe Wanderers FC and out of London as their arrangement to share with Queen's Park Rangers ends.

8TH SEP 2002

3 THE WASPS revolution that culminated in them being crowned European champions starts with this victory in the Challenge Cup, which puts them on the map!

25TH MAY 2003

4 THE CLUB from Wycombe become European champions when they beat Toulouse 27-20, Rob Howley (above) pouncing on a late mistake in the French ranks.

23RD MAY 2004

5 REVELLING ONCE again in the role of underdogs, they claim their second European title, winning the first all-English Heineken Cup final, 25-9, against arch-rivals Leicester.

20TH MAY 2007

RECORD BREAKER

Fact file

Full name: William James McBride
Date of birth: 6 June, 1940
Place of birth: Toomebridge, County Antrim, Northern Ireland
Nickname: Willie John
Position: Second-row
Test debut: 1962 v England
Test caps: 63
Test points: 4

BEHIND EVERY great team there are great leaders, men who players would follow through brick walls if asked. The best of them all was British & Irish Lions captain, the legendary Willie John McBride.

An Ulsterman, McBride came to the fore in the early 1970s when he led two of the most famous rugby teams Europe has produced: the Lions sides of 1971 and 1974.

Arguments still reign today about which of those sides was the best but what's for certain is that both of those sides were winners, the 1971 vintage winning a series in New Zealand and three years later in South Africa the 1974 Lions did the same.

A fiercely proud Irishman, McBride ended his career as the most-capped player from his country, running out in the famous Irish jersey 63 times, 11 of those appearances as captain.

But for all his endeavours for Ireland, it was his remarkable record with the Lions that made him one of the most famous rugby players ever.

Most players are happy with one Lions tour, as they only come around every few years, but McBride toured an incredible five times, more than anyone else, winning 17 caps between 1963 and 1974. That's four more than anyone in the history of rugby.

His first three tours were inauspicious and then came the two trips in the early 1970s where McBride, who only started playing rugby at 17, is credited for knitting together players from the four home nations.

The 1974 tour in particular was a violent affair as the South Africans tried to intimidate the Lions at every turn. It was McBride's toughness that got his side on top as he refused to take a backward step.

After ending his playing career in 1975, McBride coached the Ireland team and managed the 1983 Lions.

STAT ATTACK

McBride may not have won a Grand Slam but he was in the boiler room when Ireland beat South Africa for the first time, in 1965, 9-6, at the seventh attempt.

Getting ready for battle on the 1974 Lions tour

McBride toured an incredible five times with the Lions, winning 17 caps, four more than anyone else.

WILLIE JOHN McBRIDE

5 UNFORGETTABLE DAYS

1 THE TWENTY-one-year-old McBride is thrust into the Test arena, at Twickenham, having only played rugby for four years, and, even though they lose a star of Irish rugby is born.

10TH FEB 1962

2 MCBRIDE HELPS Ireland beat Australia 11-5 in Sydney, the first time a home nations team had defeated a major southern hemisphere team in their own country.

13TH MAY 1967

3 MCBRIDE'S LIONS go into the fourth and final Test against the 1971 All Blacks 2-1 up and clinch a titanic series by drawing 14-14 with New Zealand at Eden Park, Auckland.

14TH AUG 1971

4 THE SOUTH Africa series is won after the Lions take an unassailable 3-0 lead in Port Elizabeth with a 26-9 win over the Springboks, who manage to draw the final Test 13-13.

22ND JUN 1974

5 AN INCREDIBLE win for the Irish would have delighted McBride on his last game at Lansdowne Road...and he scores his only Test try in the 25-6 victory!

1ST MAR 1975

▼RECORDBREAKER▼

▼Fact file

Full name: Philippe Sella
Date of birth: 14 Feb, 1962
Place of birth: Tonneins, France
Position: Centre/Wing
First cap: 1998 v Ireland
Test caps: 111
Test points: 125

WHEN ENGLAND legend Jeremy Guscott was asked to describe what it was like to play against Philippe Sella, he said to be tackled by him was like being hit by a swinging phone box!

Sella's hits were legendary in the rugby world but he also had the soft hands of a man who was just as happy creating and scoring tries as he was stopping them.

France legend Jacques Fouroux summed Sella's abilities up best when saying he had the 'strength of a bull but the touch of a piano player'.

He also had the pace to outwit Guscott and Co and even played the first six of his seven Test matches out on the wing, finally representing his country for a staggering 13 consecutive seasons in the 1980s and 1990s.

The first rugby player in the history of the game to win 100 Test caps, he finally ended on a world-record mark of 111 when he retired at the end of the 1995 World Cup, after helping France to one final win over England in the third-place play-off.

Sella was only the fourth player in the history of the tournament to score a try in every game of a Five Nations campaign, a feat he achieved in 1986, as he played in an era when France had the flair to worry any side in the rugby world. He played through France's successful World Cup campaign in 1987 when they lost in the final to New Zealand, 29-9.

A proud representative of the Agen club for much of his career, he helped them to French championship wins in 1982 and 1988. After his Test career was concluded, Sella moved to England, once the game had turned professional, signing for Nigel Wray's Saracens along with other world stars including Francois Pienaar and Michael Lynagh. The trio inspired Saracens to a Tetley's Bitter Cup win in 1998.

Sella was inducted into the rugby Hall of Fame in 1999. Following his retirement, he set up his own marketing and communications company, and is he also a television pundit for French channel Canal+.

DID YOU KNOW?

Philippe Sella is president of 'les Enfants de l'Ovale', an educational and sporting association supporting underprivileged children (www.enfantsdelovale.org).

Sella (left) shares a joke with another Test centurion, Jason Leonard

'Sella had the strength of a bull but the touch of a piano player,' according to Jacques Fouroux.

PHILIPPE SELLA

5 UNFORGETTABLE DAYS

1 SELLA JOINS an illustrious band of players to score in every match of a Five Nations season when he crosses the line against England in Paris as the French won 29-10.

15TH MAR 1986

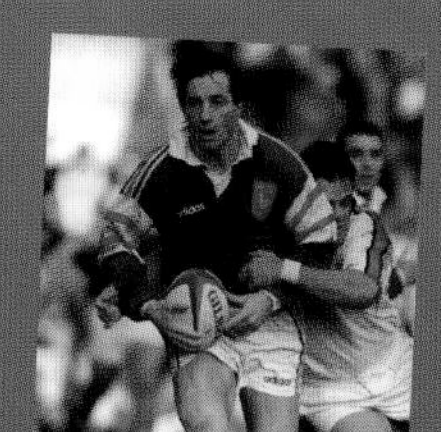

2 SELLA'S FAVOURITE try of his career comes against England in 1987 at Twickenham where the French contrive to score after an almost length-of-the-field move.

21ST FEB 1987

3 SELLA APPEARS in his only World Cup final, in 1987, but sadly for the man from Agen he was on the wrong end of a 29-9 scoreline as New Zealand lifted the trophy.

20TH JUN 1987

4 MORE THAN a tinge of sadness for Sella on his last game for France. At least it is a win, over England, but it comes in the match to avoid, the third place play-off.

22ND JUN 1995

5 OUT ON a massive high, Sella ends his career at Twickenham, as he helps his new club Saracens to lift the Tetley's Bitter Cup, beating Wasps in the final, 48-18

8TH MAR 1998

DID YOU KNOW?

The Brumbies announced that a stand is to be named after Gregan at their ground in Canberra, after he won his final game against the Crusaders.

5 UNFORGETTABLE DAYS

1 WHEN FEW people had heard of George Gregan he puts in a match-winning tackle on All Blacks wing Jeff Wilson in the Bledisloe Cup clash in 1994 to announce his arrival on the Test scene.

17TH AUG 1994

2 THE HIGH point of Gregan's career comes in Cardiff in 1999 when he lifts the Webb Ellis Cup, as Australia beat France 35-12 in the final at the Millennium Stadium.

6TH NOV 1999

3 OUTSIDE OF the Test scene Gregan is a loyal and passionate member of the ACT Brumbies, helping them to the Super 12 title in 2001, beating the Sharks.

26TH MAY 2001

4 NEW ZEALAND dominate the first decade of the Tri-Nations but in 2001 Gregan's Wallabies buck the trend, as this exceptional group of players lift the trophy.

11TH AUG 2001

5 COMING IN an incredible year for Gregan was the 2-1 series win for Australia over the British and Irish Lions. The final game was is won in Sydney by Australia, 29-23.

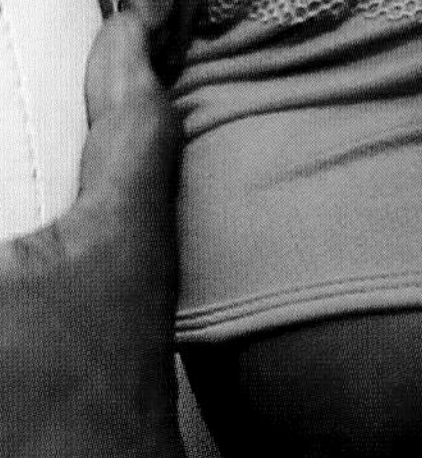

14TH JUL 2001

GEORGE GREGAN

Fact file

Full name: George Musarurwa Gregan
Date of birth: 17 May, 1973
Place of birth: Lusaka, Zambia
Height: 5ft 8in (1.73m)
Weight: 12st (76kg)
School: St. Edmund's College
Position: Scrum-half
Test debut: 1994 v Italy
Test caps: 139
Test points: 99

WHEN GEORGE Gregan walked off the field at the end of the 2007 World Cup quarter-final, it was his 139th and last game for Australia. He won a world-record number of caps, far ahead of any other player in the history of the game.

Gregan's durability was remarkable and in an outstanding career it earned him a World Cup winner's medal in 1999, Tri-Nations Championships in 2000 and 2001 and plaudits across the rugby world, not just for his scrum-half abilities but also for his leadership.

Zambian-born Gregan made his name as a combative and skilful scrum-half in the southern hemisphere's Super 12 competition, leading ACT Brumbies to the championship twice, in 2001 and 2004, and being a key reason for their success following their inception in 1996.

On the international scene a famous tackle on All Blacks wing Jeff Wilson in 1994 to stop a certain try and win a game 23-20 for Australia marked him out as a special individual destined for greatness.

But he had to wait another five years for his greatest moment on the pitch: being a key component in Australia's World Cup, vice-captain to second-row John Eales.

Two years after his World Cup win, in 2001, Gregan was part of an Australian side that won a sensational series 2-1 against the British & Irish Lions. Eales retired after the visit of the Lions and Gregan took over the captaincy of the Wallabies.

Gregan became a rugby statesman in his time at the top, forming the George Gregan (charitable) Foundation with his wife Erica after his son Max was diagnosed with epilepsy, and in 2004 he was awarded the Order of Australia for his services to rugby.

After playing his last game for Australia, Gregan started a new life in France, signing for Toulon.

Firing out the ball (below) in the last of his 139 Tests

> A remarkable career earned Gregan 139 caps, two Super 12 titles, two Tri-Nations Championships and a World Cup in 1999.

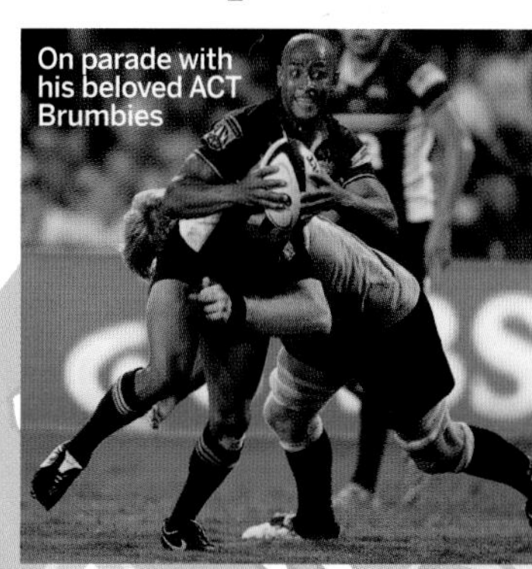

On parade with his beloved ACT Brumbies

▼TOURNAMENTS▼

GUINNESS® ESTD 1759

GUINNESS**PREMIERSHIP**

WHEN ENGLAND'S great clubs were being formed in the middle of the 19th century, they saw no need for organised leagues. A full list of friendlies against neighbouring sides, and even some with their Welsh cousins, provided all the excitement they needed, and the system developed some of the greatest English national sides in the history of the game.

But when the game began to become organised in a more professional manner in the mid-1980s it was clear that the clubs needed more than friendlies to win a new audience of supporters and those who fought against a league system were like King Canute trying to stop the tide.

In 1987 all resistance was finally broken with the establishment of the first league system sponsored by the brewers, Courage, to run alongside a National Knockout Cup competition that was started in 1972.

The Courage Leagues, the grandfather of the current Guinness Premiership, were formed within a league pyramid that had more than 1,000 clubs playing in 108 leagues – each with promotion and relegation.

Bath and Leicester were the early front runners, adapting best to the new league system. In the first ten years, only Wasps stopped Bath and Leicester dominating completely. Wasps interrupted their run by taking

▼TEAMS

THE NORTHAMPTON Saints won promotion to the Guinness Premiership in April 2008, replacing Leeds Carnegie, so for the 2008-09 season the sides in the top flight of English rugby are:

Leicester Tigers
London Wasps
Northampton Saints
Saracens
Gloucester
Bath
Worcester Warriors
Harlequins
Bristol
Newcastle
London Irish
Sale Sharks

▼FORMAT

THE GUINNESS Premiership is a 12-team league with a semi-final and final play-off at the end to determine the best team in England. The league system in England kicked off in 1987 with Courage Leagues. The Premiership has promotion and relegation (one team up and one down) with National One. In the league part of the season sides are given four points for a win and two for a draw, while a bonus point is available to any side scoring four tries in one game or finishing within seven points of the winners.

From the Courage Leagues to the Guinness Premiership, clubs have fought hard to be crowned champions of England.

Leicester won an incredible four successive English titles, here lifting the last one in 2002

the title in 1990.

The Courage League had been very popular but the league really took off when the game turned professional in 1995. Allied Dunbar took over title sponsorship from 1997-2000, and even tried to encompass the next division down by naming it Allied Dunbar Two.

Leicester were close to claiming a monopoly of the Allied Dunbar Premiership as the winner was still being decided in a straight league format without the need for play-offs, the Tigers claiming four consecutive English league titles.

With Zurich taking over the League's name, English rugby toyed with a number of different play-off structures, at one point awarding a trophy to the side that finished top of the table at the end of the regular season and another to the one that won the play-offs! They also allowed eight teams into a muddled play-off format and it was only when the league became the Guinness Premiership in 2005-06 that the structure settled down. Now the top four sides move into the end-of-season play-offs, with a semi-final and a final to determine the winner.

DID YOU KNOW?

The original members of the top flight of English rugby, Courage Div One, in 1987 were: Bath, Bristol, Coventry, Gloucester, Harlequins, Leicester, Moseley, Nottingham, Orrell, Sale (right), Wasps, Waterloo.

ENGLISH KNOCKOUT CUP

It kicked off in 1972...the last four winners

Ospreys captain Ryan Jones

2008

THE 2008 final of the EDF Energy Cup was a repeat of the 2007 final but with the opposite result. The Ospreys overwhelming the Leicester Tigers, with tries from Andrew Bishop and second-row Alun Wyn Jones.

Tom Varndell celebrates the win

2007

THE SECOND Anglo Welsh tournament was won by the Leicester Tigers as they won a thrilling final at Twickenham 41-35 against the Ospreys, two tries coming from Leicester flyer Tom Varndell, in front of 60,000 spectators.

2006 Matt Dawson

LONDON WASPS broke new ground by winning in the new Anglo Welsh format, with teams in four pools, against the Llanelli Scarlets 26-10, Tom Voyce scoring both of Wasps' tries, before a 57,212-strong Twickenham crowd.

Iain Balshaw is rightly delighted

2005

LEEDS INFLICTED the first defeat on Bath in an English cup final, this time to claim the Powergen Cup and a coveted place in Europe. Tries from Chris Bell and Andre Snyman were enough to put Leeds in control at half time and they ran out 20-12 victors, for one of the proudest days in the club's history. Bath only managing to get on the scoreboard through the boot of Chris Malone, while Gordon Ross replied with 10 points of his own.

DID YOU KNOW?

Home and away fixtures in Courage Division One were introduced in 1993-94

Lawrence Dallaglio led London Wasps to the Guinness Premiership title in 2008

TIME TO PLAY

MAGNERS LEAGUE

MAGNERS LEAGUE RECORDS

OSPREYS

LEINSTER

The fiercely contested Celtic League kicked off in 2001 and, through various formats, produced a number of winners.

2001-02: Celtic League
Winners: Leinster
Final: Leinster 24 Munster 20

2002-03: Celtic League
Winners: Munster
Final: Munster 37 Neath 17

2003-04: Celtic League
Winners: Llanelli Scarlets
*League system only

2004-05: Celtic League
Winners: Ospreys
*League system only

2004-05: Celtic Cup
Winners: Munster
Final: Munster 27 Llanelli 16
*Top eight sides in League

2005-06: Celtic League
Winners: Ulster
*League system only

2006-07: Magners League
Winners: Ospreys
*League system only

2007-08: Magners League
Winners: Leinster
*League system only

MUNSTER

EDINBURGH

DID YOU KNOW?
There is a league within a league in the Magners set-up as they also run the Specsavers Fairplay League, rewarding the club with the best disciplinary record, with £10,000 to spend on their youth development.

THE CELTIC countries of Wales, Scotland and Ireland were slow out of the blocks when professionalism hit rugby union like a rocket out of the sky in 1995, and they took longer than any other of the major nations to get organised into a league.

The three countries were content in the mid-1990s to keep their domestic leagues, but it was clear they would need to develop a cross-border competition when it was apparent they had missed the chance to link up with either England or France.

In fact, it took them until 2001 to band together under the Celtic League banner. In those days there were 15 teams in the League as Wales entered nine club sides, but that changed in 2003-04 when Wales introduced regional rugby in the country.

Brewery Field hosted the first-ever match between Bridgend and Pontypridd, which the visitors won 27-19, whilst Pontypridd's Richard Johnston scored the first ever league try after 10 minutes. At the time the league was based in pools, moving into a quarter-final, semi-final and final before the inaugural final was staged at Lansdowne Road on 15 December 2001, where 30,000 fans saw Leinster defeat Munster 24-20.

In 2003-03 the league was expanded to 16 teams, and a new bonus-point structure was added, with the introduction of a third Scottish side, the Borders. But the teams only met once in the season.

In this second season a play-off system was still in existence, the quarter-finals, between the top four finishers in each pool, following in late November. The second final took place at Millennium Stadium on 1 February 2003 and saw Munster defeat Neath 37-17 in front of more than 30,000 spectators.

In 2003-04 the revolution taking place in Welsh rugby impinged on the Celtic League, with their five new regions taking up their places in a 12-team league, playing each other home and away for the first time in a 22-week league over the entire season.

The Celtic League struggled to find its place in the rugby world but the competition took a huge step forwards when its first title sponsor arrived in 2006-07 to name the new Magners League. Ulster won the first Magners League and, with the Welsh sides settled, the matches took on a much more meaningful look, the Ospreys taking the second title.

DID YOU KNOW?
There is no promotion to or relegation from the Magners League, operating like the Super 14.

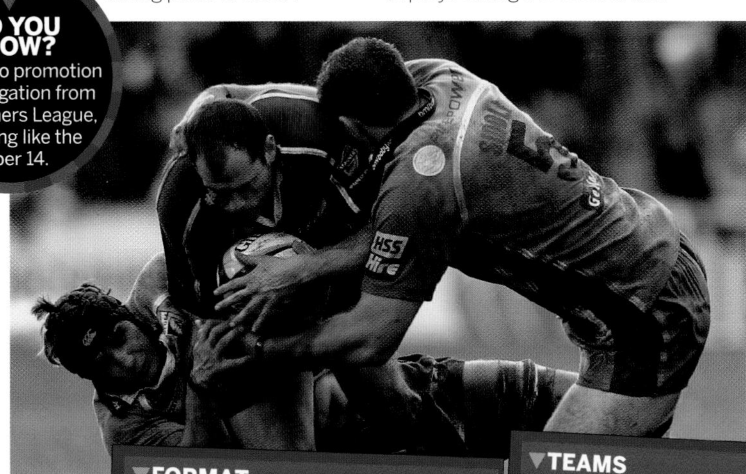

The best club, regional and provincial sides of Wales, Scotland and Ireland collide in the new Magners League.

FORMAT

EACH TEAM plays every other team in the tournament twice a season on a home and away basis. In all matches, four points are awarded for a win and two for a draw.

A team scoring four or more tries in a game is awarded a bonus point, while another bonus point is also awarded to any team losing by seven points or less.

The winner and all placings in the Magners League will be decided on the number of league points. If two or more teams have the same number of points their placings will be determined by the following basis in descending order: number of matches won; points difference; number of tries scored.

TEAMS

WITH THE demise of the Borders side, the League was left with 10 teams for the 2008-09 season:

Wales
Cardiff Blues
Llanelli Scarlets
Newport Gwent Dragons
The Ospreys
Scotland
Edinburgh
Glasgow
Ireland
Munster
Connacht
Leinster
Ulster

TOURNAMENTS

SUPER 14

WITH SOUTH Africa banned from international sporting competition at the start of the 1990s, due to their apartheid political regime, it was left to the other major nations in the southern hemisphere to kick off the era of Super rugby, organised for regions to play each other rather than clubs.

Today it is the world-famous Super 14 competition, pitting the best regions or franchises from New Zealand, Australia and South Africa against each other. But when it started in 1992 it was just a Super 6 competition, encompassing teams from New South Wales, Queensland, Fiji, Auckland, Canterbury and Wellington.

Professionalism changed the face of Super rugby forever and, when the game ditched its amateur past in 1995, the tournament was quickly renamed the Super 12 with three teams from Australia, four from South Africa and five from New Zealand making up this new competition.

Pioneers of the end-of-season play-offs and bonus-point system, which adds points for sides scoring more than four tries and finishing within seven points of the winners, Super rugby led the way in terms of non-international competition after 1995.

The Super 12 quickly defined its own style, where massive points scores were common. Criticism arrived from the northern hemisphere, where it was felt that Super rugby was not preparing players for Test rugby. But the south remained confident in their competition and it went from strength to strength, although disappointingly for many

STAT ATTACK

Winners: **1996:** Auckland Blues, **1997:** Auckland **1998, 99 & 2000:** Crusaders, **2001:** Brumbies, **2002:** Crusaders, **2003:** Blues, **2004:** Brumbies, **2005 & 06:** Crusaders, **2007:** Bulls, **2008:** Crusaders.

The Super 14, which runs from February to May each year, sets the tone for the rugby season in the southern hemisphere countries.

TEAMS

Crusaders – From Canterbury (NZ)
Brumbies – From The ACT (Aus)
Waratahs – From New S.Wales (Aus)
Reds – From Queensland (Aus)
Western Force – From Perth (Aus)
Blues – From Auckland (NZ)
Chiefs – From Waikato (NZ)
Highlanders – From Dunedin (NZ)
Hurricanes – From Wellington (NZ)
Bulls – From Pretoria (SA)
Cheetahs – From Bloemfontein (SA)
Lions – From Johannesburg (SA)
Sharks – From Durban (SA)
Stormers – From Cape Town (SA)

FORMAT

THE SUPER 14 is a round-robin competition where each team plays every other team once; a team has six or seven home games, and six or seven away games each. There are 91 regular-season games in total. Games are held over 14 weekends with each team receiving one bye. The Super 14 uses the rugby union bonus points system. The top four teams at the end of the round-robin phase then play semi-finals. The first-placed team hosts the fourth-placed team, and the second-placed team hosts the third-placed team. The two winners then play the final at the home ground of the top surviving seed.

SUPER 14 RECORDS

WARATAHS

Records seem to tumble in the Super 14 every season. Here are some of the great feats of rugby:

Highest score:
96 – Crusaders v Waratahs (19), 2002

Lowest score:
0 – Bulls v Brumbies (15), '99; Cats v Brumbies (64), 2000; Bulls v Highlanders (23), 2005; Brumbies v Blues (17), 2006; Reds v Brumbies (36), 2007; Force v Crusaders (53)

Highest winning margin:
89 – Bulls v Reds (92-3), 2007

Highest score away:
60 – Blues v Hurricanes (7), 2002

Most consecutive wins:
15 – Crusaders, 2002-03

Most consecutive losses:
11 – Bulls, 2002

Most tries in a match:
14 – Crusaders v Waratahs, 2002

Most tries in a season:
71 – Crusaders, 2005

Most wins in a season:
12 – Crusaders, 2008 regular season

Most points in a season:
221 – Dan Carter for the Crusaders in 2006

Fewest wins in a season:
0 – Bulls, 2002 regular season

First Super rugby try:
Alama Ieremia, Blues v Hurricanes, Palmerston North, 1996

Thanks to www.super14.com for these statistics

BLUES

DID YOU KNOW?
The most points in a Super rugby final is 85 in 2004 as the Brumbies beat the Crusaders

BULLS

THE FORCE

commentators they have never embraced their near neighbours of Samoa, Tonga or the founding country of Fiji. Even when the Super 12 became the Super 14 in 2007, the South Sea Islands were ignored and an extra side from both Australia and South Africa were added to make up the numbers.

Sides from New Zealand have dominated the competition as they have with the Tri-Nations, Kiwi teams winning 10 of the first 12 competitions. South Africa had to wait until 2007 to win their first title, by the Bryan Habana-inspired Bulls, who beat the Sharks in an all-South African final, setting the tone for the World Cup, that year.

It was the Auckland Blues who were in the ascendancy in the early years while the Canterbury Crusaders broke the mould, winning three consecutive titles from 1998.

Controversy reigned in 2007 when New Zealand's international coach Graham Henry decided to rest many of his All Blacks players from the early rounds of the Super 14, thereby undermining the tournament.

In 2008, with all sides back at full strength, the Crusaders finished on top of the table in the regular season, going on to beat the Waratahs 20-12 in the final, for their seventh title, 15 points from Dan Carter and a try from Mose Tuiali'i sealing it.

DID YOU KNOW?
The first Heineken Cup in 1995 had 12 teams from Ireland, Wales, Italy, Romania and France.

HEINEKEN CUP

The greatest prize in European club rugby is only won by the best sides.

THE FIRST 13 FINALS

1996: Toulouse (Fra) 21 Cardiff 18
1997: Brive (Fra) 28 Leicester 9
1998: Bath (Eng) 19 Brive 18
1999: Ulster (Irel) 21 Colomiers 6
2000: Northampton (Eng) 9 Munster 8
2001: Leicester (Eng) 34 Stade Français 30
2002: Leicester (Eng) 15 Munster 9
2003: Toulouse (Fra) 22 Perpignan 17
2004: Wasps (Eng) 27 Toulouse 20
2005: Toulouse (Fra) 18 Stade Francais 12
2006: Munster (Irel) 23 Biarritz 19
2007: Wasps (Eng) 25 Leicester 9
2008: Munster (Irel) 16 Toulouse 13

FORMAT

THE HEINEKEN Cup is open to clubs in the Magners League (Wales, Scotland and Ireland), Guinness Premiership (England), Super 10 (Italy) and the Top 14 (France). From the 2008-09 season the sides will be ranked according to a complicated seedings system based on their last few years in the tournament. The 24 sides are placed into six pools with the winners and two best runners-up qualifying for the quarter-finals. In matches four points are awarded for a win and two points for a draw. A bonus point is awarded for a loss by seven points or fewer, or for scoring four tries.

IT ALL started in the humble surroundings of the Romanian Black Sea resort of Constanta back on 31st October 1995, but today the Heineken Cup is the most prized club trophy in Europe.

Back in 1995 when it kicked off with Toulouse's 54-10 win over Farul Constanta, not everyone was convinced there would be a future for a pan-European cup competition. Was a British league, a European league or various domestic competitions the best way forward? But as the game has learnt to cope with the changes that professionalism has brought. The Heineken Cup, which was the initiative of the then-Five Nations Committee, has stood out like a beacon for those who love the game of rugby.

Although the Romanians were there in all their glory in 1995, the competition has been pared down since its start and now has clubs and provinces from England, Wales, Scotland, Ireland, Italy and France with a second-ranked competition, the European Challenge Cup, catering for the developing nations.

In just 10 years since then it has taken European rugby by storm, catching the imagination of players and supporters like a forest fire. Attendances in 2005 totalled a record 920,239, a massive 103,872 more than the old mark set a year earlier, while it is also the vital higher stepping stone between domestic tournaments and the international stage.

DID YOU KNOW?

Due to a ban on alcohol advertising of any kind in France the tournament in France is called the H-Cup, but known throughout rest of the rugby world as the Heineken Cup, since its kick-off in 1995.

The games have increased in intensity since the kick-off and now many of the games would rank in terms of ability with Test matches. Unlike the Super 14, its counterpart in the southern hemisphere, the Heineken Cup is not played in one block in Europe, instead fitting its matches around club tournaments, November Test matches and the Six Nations Championship. Therefore first games are normally played in October, with the final in May.

England and France have dominated the tournament although Munster's win in 2006 and Ulster's in 1999, when the English clubs staged a boycott, broke the duopoly.

Toulouse became the first club to win the coveted Heineken Cup three times when they beat Stade Français Paris 18-12 in an all-French final at Murrayfield in 2005.

The 10th anniversary season of European club rugby's premier tournament turned into a triumph for coach Guy Noves – who guided Toulouse to that unique treble in 1996, 2003 and 2005 – and captain Fabien Pelous.

In 2008 Munster were once again crowned kings of Europe.

HEINEKEN CUP RECORDS

The shocks, sensations and triumphs in Europe

2005

2006

2007

2008

After the 2008 final here are some Heineken Cup Final snapshots, courtesy of European Rugby Cup:

- Munster became the fourth team to win the Heineken Cup twice, joining Toulouse (three wins), Leicester Tigers and London Wasps.
- This was the 10th out of the 13 finals to have been won by the margin of less than a converted try.
- Munster became the third team to play in four Heineken Cup finals, joining Toulouse (five) and Leicester Tigers (four).
- Overall, the first 13 finals have produced 23 tries – an average of 1.77 – with two players scoring braces, Sebastien Carrat (Brive, 1997) and Leon Lloyd (Leicester, 2001).
- The 79 matches in the 2008-09 season produced 356 tries and were watched by 942,373 fans – match averages of 4.50 and 11,929 respectively.
- A total of 719,015 fans went through the turnstiles for the 13 Heineken Cup finals, an average of 55,308 per final.

And finally ... Toulouse won the first final in 1996, in front of 21,800 fans at Cardiff Arms Park and in 2008 an incredible 74,500 supporters packed into the Millennium Stadium for the final against Munster.

DID YOU KNOW?

Martin Johnson is a massive American Football fan, playing for the Leicester Panthers, and commentating, on the Super Bowl for Channel 4.

5 UNFORGETTABLE DAYS

16TH JAN 1993

1 AN INJURY to Wade Dooley gives Johnson a dramatic and unexpected England debut in 1993, but true to form he performs superbly as England win 16-15, Ian Hunter scoring the try.

28TH JUN 1997

2 JOHNSON IS just as prodigious in a Lions shirt, leading them to a sensational 2-1 series win in 1997.

19TH MAY 2001

3 JOHNNO WAS a fiercely proud Leicester Tiger so their 34-30 Heineken Cup final win over Stade Francais in 2001 ranks up there with anything he did in Test matches. A great leader.

14TH JUNE 2003

4 JOHNSON IS a crucial part of England's 15-13 win in New Zealand in 2003, only their second ever in that country.

22ND NOV 2003

5 JOHNSON BECOMES the first man from the northern hemisphere to lift the World Cup, after a dramatic win over Australia. Many credited him with inspiring the last efforts.

Commanding the lineout for Leicester

MARTIN JOHNSON

IT IS almost impossible in a team game like rugby to name the greatest player of all time but Leicester, England and Lions captain Martin Johnson would be at the head of most polls.

An inspirational leader, Johnson led by example, never asking anyone to do something he wouldn't do himself, bringing almost unheard-of success to his club, country and the British & Irish Lions, and maintaining his standards as a world-class player for more than a decade at the top.

Feared throughout the rugby world, Johnson was so motivated to become a world-class player that he headed off to New Zealand as a teenager, using the country's rugged landscape as a rugby finishing school. While there, he was even selected for the country's under-21 side and All Blacks great Colin Meads tried to convince the young tyro to stay. But Johnson's heart always belonged to Blighty and back he came to start one of the most impressive careers rugby has ever known. He didn't score tries like Rory Underwood or kick points like Jonny Wilkinson, but Johnson was the one player you would rather have with you than against you.

> 'You saw Martin Johnson at his absolute best in that 10-minute period. His leadership was just inspirational,' said Clive Woodward.

Fact file

Full name: Martin Osborne Johnson
Date of birth: 9 March, 1970
Place of birth: Solihull, West Mids United Kingdom
Height: 6ft 7in (2.01 m)
Weight: 18st 10lbs (119kg)
School: Robert Smyth School
Position: Second row
First cap: 1993 v France
Test caps (for England): 84

There are many highlights in his illustrious career but the game that set the platform for the famous World Cup victory came a couple of months earlier in New Zealand.

Down to six forwards, and with Neil Back and Lawrence Dallaglio in the sin-bin, Johnson ensured the All Blacks would not pass for only England's second win in New Zealand. 'You saw Martin at his absolute best in that 10-minute period,' said coach Clive Woodward.

While captain, as well as the World Cup victory, he led the Lions to a 2-1 series win against the then-world champions, South Africa, and inspired his beloved Leicester Tigers to unparalleled success as they won back-to-back Heineken Cups and the Zurich Premiership an incredible four times around the turn of the century.

In 2008 Johnson was appointed England Team Manager.

In the lineout...

...on the run

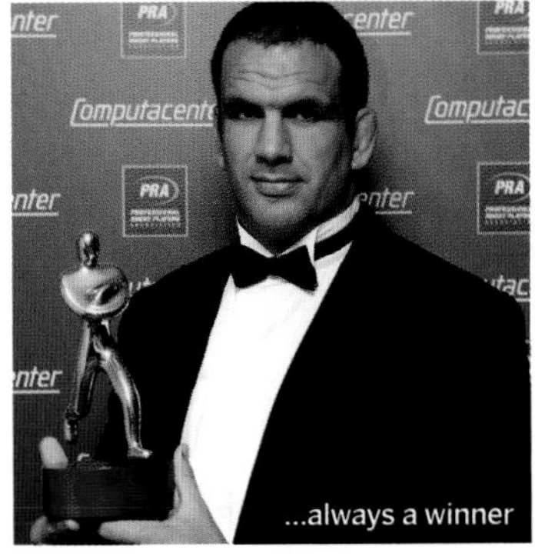

...always a winner

SA RUGBY

FRANCOIS PIENAAR

'No Hollywood scriptwriter could have written a better script.' Francois Pienaar on his greatest day.

Fact file

Full name: Jacobus Francois Pienaar
Date of birth: 2 January, 1967
Place of birth: Vereeniging,
Height: 6ft 3in (1.91m)
Weight: 17st (108kg)
Position: Flanker
First cap: 1993 v France
Test caps: 29, and 15 Test points

IN MODERN-day rugby it is no longer unusual to see a player win 70 or 80 caps, so it seems remarkable that a man with just 29 to his name could have made such an impact on the game.

But Francois Pienaar was no ordinary rugby player, uniting a nation as both South Africa and the game of rugby union were in turmoil. An uncompromising flanker, Pienaar was captain of one of the most famous teams in rugby history: The 1995 Springboks.

The historic moment between Pienaar and President Mandela

The country, which is steeped in rugby history, had been banned from international sporting competition in the 1980s due to its apartheid political regime (which separated black and white people). They roared back into competition in 1992 with Pienaar at the helm, hosting the World Cup three years later and with a certain inevitability stormed to the final, winning it in extra time (from a Joel Stransky drop goal) 15-12, and stopping Jonah Lomu in the process.

Their perfect day was crowned when South Africa's President Nelson Mandela presented Pienaar with the trophy wearing a green shirt exactly the same as the rugby player. 'I've said it many times that no Hollywood scriptwriter could have written a better script,' Pienaar recalls. 'It was just unbelievable on the streets of South Africa. For the first time all the people had come together and all races and religions were hugging each other. Nelson Mandela then said to me, 'thank you very much for what you've done for South Africa,' but I said, 'thank you for what you've done'.

When the game turned professional after the 1995 World Cup, Pienaar, by now one of the game's statesmen, was one of the rugby superstars to seek a new life in England. He joined Nigel Wray's Saracens and won the Tetley's Bitter Cup in 1998, the club's first major trophy for 127 years.

After retiring from playing, he became Chief Executive at Saracens and even fronted South Africa's bid to host the 2011 World Cup.

DID YOU KNOW?

Pienaar made his name in South Africa as part of the great Transvaal side. He made his first-class rugby debut for them in 1989, winning 100 caps.

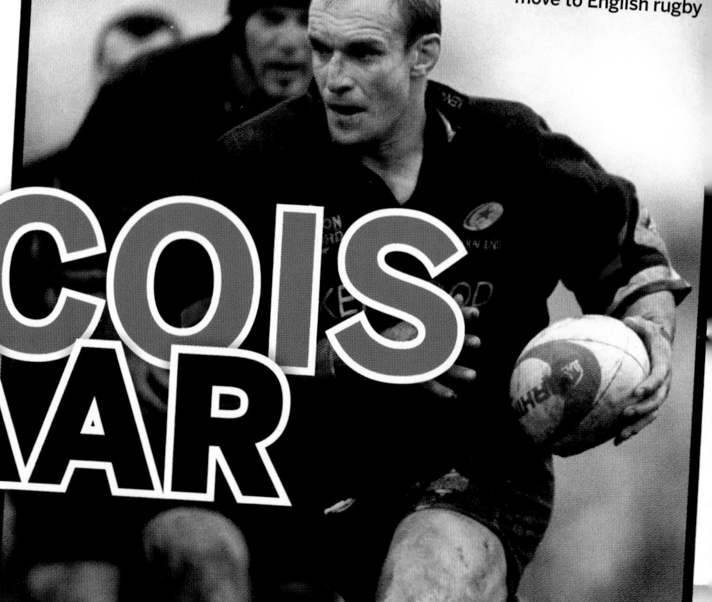
Pienaar was one of the first global stars to move to English rugby

5 UNFORGETTABLE DAYS

1 FRANCOIS PIENAAR makes his South Africa debut as captain in 1993 and inspires his side to a 20-20 draw with France in Durban, before going on to lose the second game.

26TH JUN 1993

2 AFTER TWO defeats in New Zealand, Pienaar's side give themselves hope for the World Cup with a 18-18 draw in Auckland. It is a huge morale boost.

6TH AUG 1994

3 AN INCREDIBLE World Cup victory in front of his own fans, 15-12 over New Zealand. 'We did not have 63,000 fans behind us today, we had 43 million South Africans,' he says.

24TH JUN 1995

4 AFTER THE World Cup he took his Springboks back to Twickenham, winning 24-14 in front of a capacity 75,000 crowd, crowning a sensational year for him, and the Boks.

18TH NOV 1995

5 AFTER JOINING English club Saracens with a number of other stars, Pienaar is instrumental in them winning the 1998 Tetley's Bitter Cup.

9TH MAY 1998

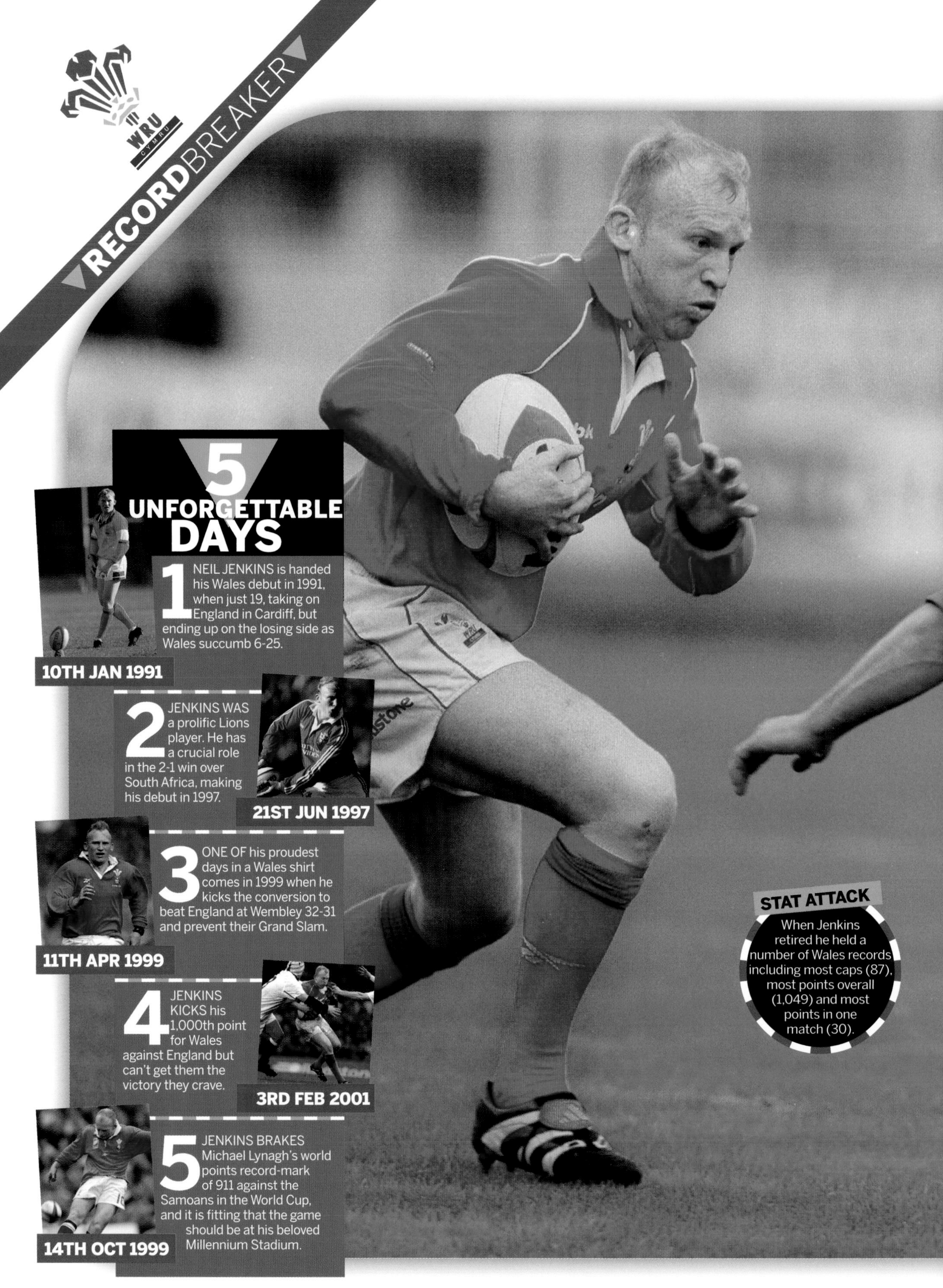

WRU CYMRU

RECORD BREAKER

5 UNFORGETTABLE DAYS

1 NEIL JENKINS is handed his Wales debut in 1991, when just 19, taking on England in Cardiff, but ending up on the losing side as Wales succumb 6-25.

10TH JAN 1991

2 JENKINS WAS a prolific Lions player. He has a crucial role in the 2-1 win over South Africa, making his debut in 1997.

21ST JUN 1997

3 ONE OF his proudest days in a Wales shirt comes in 1999 when he kicks the conversion to beat England at Wembley 32-31 and prevent their Grand Slam.

11TH APR 1999

4 JENKINS KICKS his 1,000th point for Wales against England but can't get them the victory they crave.

3RD FEB 2001

5 JENKINS BRAKES Michael Lynagh's world points record-mark of 911 against the Samoans in the World Cup, and it is fitting that the game should be at his beloved Millennium Stadium.

14TH OCT 1999

STAT ATTACK

When Jenkins retired he held a number of Wales records including most caps (87), most points overall (1,049) and most points in one match (30).

NEIL JENKINS

Simply the best...Only Wilkinson has scored more points than Jenks

The man with the Golden Boot set records almost everywhere he went, ending his career with more Test points than anyone in history.

NICKNAMED THE Ginger Monster, Neil Jenkins is one of the most prolific goalkickers the rugby world has seen. When he finally hung up his international boots in 2002 after the Romania game, the lad from the Rhondda Valley had scored a world-record 1,090 points for Wales and the British & Irish Lions.

Jenkins was the first player to score 1,000 Test points and his world record stood until 2008, when Jonny Wilkinson overtook his mark in the RBS 6 Nations clash with Scotland.

Jenkins certainly didn't achieve his records the easy way. Criticised for much of his career as Wales No 10, he battled adversity to end as a much-loved son of the Welsh nation. He developed not only his goalkicking but, after a lot of hard work, his distribution, game management and tactical awareness.

Making his Wales debut as a teenager, he suffered badly in comparison with some of the greats, like Barry John, Phil Bennett and Jonathan Davies, who had worn the shirt before him but, like those legends, he was a winner.

Jenkins played for Pontypridd, Cardiff and Celtic Warriors in an illustrious club career. His versatility was proved on the Lions tour to South Africa in 1997, when he played full-back in all three Tests as the British & Irish side won 2-1, scoring 41 of his 1,090 Test points for the Lions. His goalkicking again was crucial, not just in the Test matches but to ignite the Lions campaign in the provincial games.

Jenkins followed up his selection in 1997 by making the tour to Australia four years later, although injury robbed him of the chance to make a claim for a Test shirt Down Under.

Jenkins battled back from his injuries to make a sustained case for inclusion in Wales' 2003 World Cup squad. But when coach Steve Hansen rejected his bid he decided to retire, going out on a high with a testimonial match at the Millennium Stadium watched by 40,000 people. It ended in an 80-80 draw!

Fact file

Full name: Neil Robert Jenkins
Date of birth: 8 July, 1971
Place of birth: Church Village,
Height: 5ft 10in (1.78m)
Weight: 13st 8lbs (86kg)
Nickname: Ginger Monster
Position: Fly-half, Full-Back
First cap: 1991 v England
Test caps (Wales): 87
Test points (Wales): 1,049

Whether on the field for...

Wales or...

the Lions, Jenkins was much-loved

YOUNGGUNS

Young players are the lifeblood of any sport and in rugby union there is an exciting new crop ready to rule the roost. Here are six of the best!

TEEN TEST

The youngest player to take the field for Wales was way back in 1889, when aged just 18 years and 119 days, Norman Biggs represented his country.

ROBERT FRUEAN
NEW ZEALAND | THE HURRICANES

6 THE International Rugby Board's Young Player of the Year in 2007, Kiwi centre Robert Fruean has already made a big impact in his short career at the top. The Wellingtonian won his award on the back of an outstanding World Under-19 tournament in 2007, when he led the Baby Blacks to the title in Belfast. The talented centre launched himself through his performances for the Wellington Lions in the Air New Zealand Cup, making an impact on the world stage at the championship, most notably scoring two tries as New Zealand won the final 31-7 against South Africa. Fruean has already had to overcome some health problems, but got his first steps on the ladder when the Porirua College head boy earned a scholarship from the First Foundation.

KURTLEY BEALE
AUSTRALIA | WARATAHS

5 ALREADY ONE of the most talented players in the Super 14, Kurtley Beale was a schoolboy star, who is starting to show his worth in adult rugby. Beale, who started his rugby career in league, made his Super 14 debut in 2007, just two months after completing his Higher School Certificate qualification. The Mazda Australian Rugby Championship Player of the Tournament in 2007, Beale won the award playing for the Western Sydney Rams. He was signed by the Super 14 franchise, the Waratahs when he was only a 16-year-old but has already spent his young career surrounded by speculation that he may one day leave union behind him and return to league. Captain of the Australian schoolboys side, comparisons with Mark Ella (one of Australia's greatest ever outside-halves) have already been made, as Beale made the Waratahs No 10 shirt his own in 2008.

4 LUKE FITZGERALD is the brightest young star on the Irish rugby scene since a certain Brian O'Driscoll broke through in an unforgettable way in the late 1990s. Much like O'Driscoll, Fitzgerald studied at Blackrock College, and plays centre, while his father (Des) had an illustrious rugby career, also playing for Ireland. The 2005 Irish Examiner Young Rugby Player of the Year, Fitzgerald junior won his first cap for Ireland in November 2006 against the Pacific Islands, after long being marked out as a player who could go all the way to the top. He missed out on the 2007 World Cup, but has the ability to be one of the first names on the team sheet in 2011 as he is just as much at home on the wing or at full-back. At 19 he was the youngest player to represent Ireland since 1977.

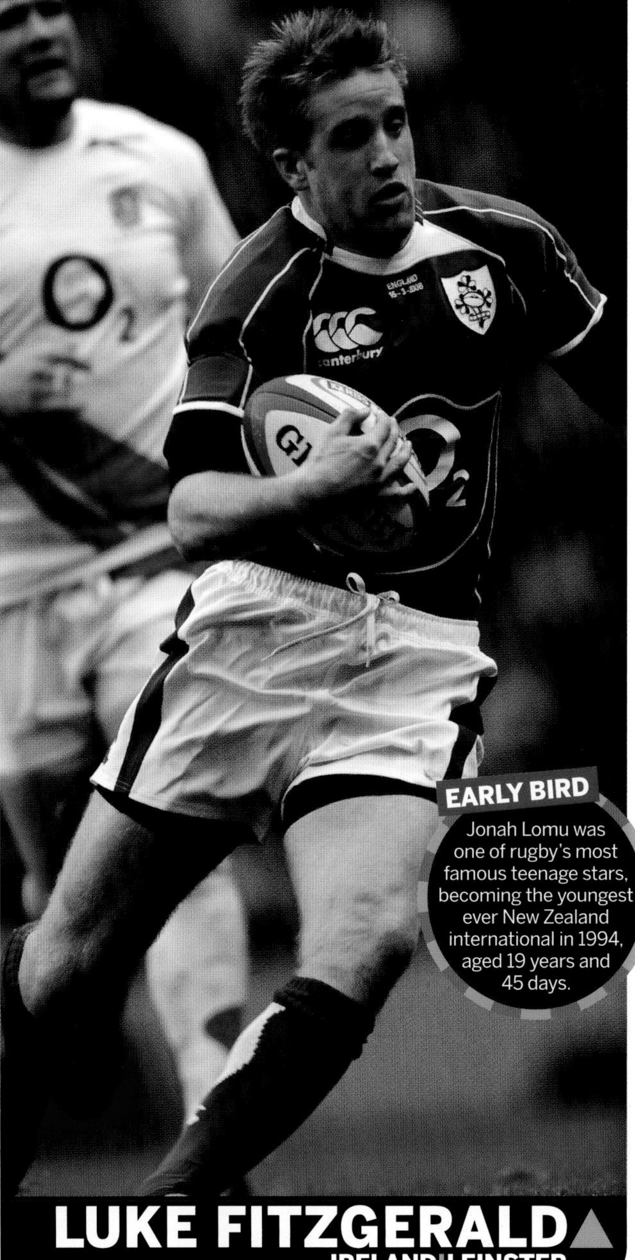

EARLY BIRD

Jonah Lomu was one of rugby's most famous teenage stars, becoming the youngest ever New Zealand international in 1994, aged 19 years and 45 days.

LUKE FITZGERALD
IRELAND | LEINSTER

FRANCOIS TRINH-DUC

FRANCE | MONTPELLIER

3 IN THE 2008 RBS 6 Nations, France capped a number of bright young stars, but one who could establish himself most easily is Montpellier outside-half François Trinh-Duc. Of Vietnamese origin, Trinh-Duc put himself in the spotlight with some startling performances in the Top 14 when his flair and lack of fear marked him out as a player who could emerge as France's outside-half for many years to come. He won his first cap as a 21-year-old, after taking up the game as a four-year-old in Montpellier, confirming his pedigree. A former scrum-half, Trinh-Duc won his first cap after just 16 games for his club, symbolising a new-look France team that emerged after the disappointment of finishing fourth, playing a narrow game plan, in the World Cup. He believes attack comes first, more in the style of the great French sides of the 1970s and 1980s.

TOM JAMES

WALES | CARDIFF BLUES

2 WITH SPEED to burn, Cardiff wing Tom James has had a whirlwind start to his regional and international career, and has been marked out as a player who could have a long stay at the very top level. A former international middle-distance runner, James committed himself to rugby, first with Merthyr Tydfil RFC, before moving to Cardiff RFC and quickly into the Cardiff Blues regional set-up. Eleven tries in nine games for Cardiff made a huge impact and elevated him to the Blues. James got his international chance in the summer of 2007 when he was called into Wales' squad for the tour of Australia, finally making his Test debut against England in August. He marked his Cardiff Blues debut with a try, also enjoying a season with the Wales Sevens.

DANNY CIPRIANI

ENGLAND | LONDON WASPS

Fact file

Full name: Danny Cipriani
Date of birth: Nov 2, 1987
Place of birth: Roehampton England
Height: 6ft (1.84m)
Weight: 14st 3lbs (90kg)
Nickname: Cips
School: Whitgift School
Position: Fly-half
First cap: 2008 v Wales at Twickenham

1 THE TWENTY-year-old who took the England No 10 shirt from Jonny Wilkinson, Danny Cipriani is one of the most naturally gifted players ever to wear the red rose. A replacement in the Wales and Italy games in 2008, he finally won his battle with Wilkinson to start the Test against Ireland. A natural leader, he isn't afraid to bark orders at players with years more experience at the top level. A veteran of two World Championships, both with England U19s, he started rugby at the age of nine, joining Rosslyn Park U10s, making his Wasps debut aged 17 against Bristol. An impressive goalkicker, he is a big attacking threat, and showed his versatility playing full-back as Wasps beat Leicester in the 2007 Heineken Cup final. In May 2008 he broke his ankle playing for Wasps taking him out of England's tour to New Zealand.

YOUNG FUN

The youngest player ever to win a cap for England was Henry Laird, back in 1927, who made his debut aged just 18 years and 152 days.

Almost one million England fans packed into central London to celebrate the country's World Cup win in 2003

FANS OF THE WORLD

RUGBY SUPPORTERS are some of the most passionate sports fans in the world, with more than 30,000 expected to travel to South Africa in 2009 to follow the British and Irish Lions. They come in all shapes and sizes as the next few pages show and, although they enjoy a drink or two, they are some of the most friendly fans on the planet. Marvel at their get-ups and laugh at their antics as we pay homage to the fans of the great game of rugby. ▶

These Scotland fans make sure you get the message

Anyone call for a band?

Even when New Zealand lost in 2007, the fans stayed loyal

Now that is commitment to the Italian team!

Fans of Saracens and the Ospreys join together

You can never find a pen when you need one!

FANS OF THE WORLD

Wales fans travel in their thousands to every match

Green is the only way to go for the Irish supporters

Spiderman and his friend enjoy the rugby

Scotland v England is sealed with a kiss!

Perhaps the guy above might just support the mighty Fijian team?

It's passion all the way with the supporters of Biarritz

These two groups of France fans know how to have a good time

ACKNOWLEDGEMENTS

NO BOOK of this nature could ever come together without recourse to a number of the magnificent resources contained within the great game of rugby union.

Unlike when I produced my first history of rugby almost 10 years ago, the internet is now a great source of information. Websites such as planet-rugby.com, super14.com, the BBC's excellent sports sites and rugbyworld.com were a great help, as was the greatly improved irb.com and the official sites of the clubs and unions we featured in these pages.

Newspapers are a great unsung source as well. Leading the way in rugby terms are *The Daily Telegraph*, *The Sunday Telegraph*, *The Times* and *The Sunday Times*.

In the world of rugby statistics, there are a number of books that I have always regarded as a great shoulder to lean on, and there are some great statisticians out there, such as John Griffiths, Jed Smith, Stuart Farmer and Bob Howitt. My thanks go to a number of different volumes, including:

* *The IRB World Rugby Yearbook 2007 & 08*: John Griffiths (Vision Sport Publishing)
* *75 New Zealand Rugby Greats:* Bob Howitt (Hodder Moa Beckett)
* *The History of the Lions:* Clem & Greg Thomas (Mainstream)
* *Springbok Rugby:* Chris Greystein (New Holland Publishers)
* *Daily Telegraph's History of Rugby* (Telegraph Books)
* *Men in Black:* Rod Chester, Ron Palenski (Hodder Boa Beckett)
* *The Rugby Miscellany series* with various writers (Vision Sport Publishing)

This book is endorsed by the RFU. If you have any comments about the book, email me at *Rugby World* on paul_morgan@ipcmedia.com. I would be particularly interested in any rugby history or reference books you have enjoyed.